I0814454

THE DESIGN OF YOU

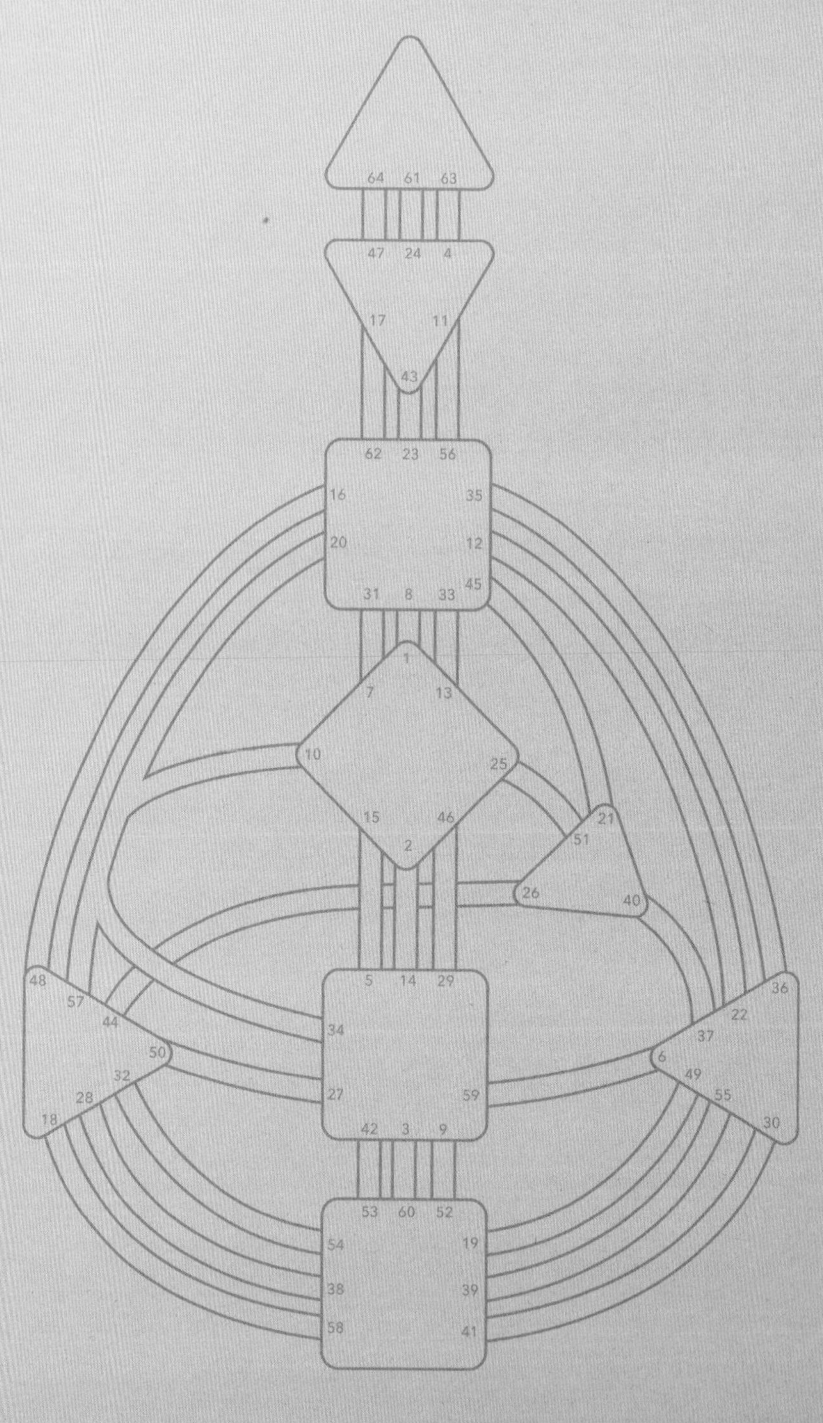
64 61 63
47 24 4
17 11
43
62 23 56
16 35
20 12
45
31 8 33
1
7 13
10 25
15 46
2
21
51
26
40
48
57
44
50
32
28
18
5 14 29
34
27 59
42 3 9
36
22
37
6
49
55
30
53 60 52
54 19
38 39
58 41

Leah McCloud

The DESIGN *of* YOU

Using Human Design to Manifest Your Dream

Life · Love · Career

CHRONICLE PRISM

Dedicated to all who seek to understand themselves deeply.
May this book light your path to self-discovery.

Copyright © 2025 by Leah McCloud

All rights reserved. No part of this book may be reproduced in any form without written permission from the publisher.

Library of Congress Cataloging-in-Publication Data available.

ISBN 978-1-7972-3378-9
LCCN 2025017690

Manufactured in China.

Interior design by Pamela Geismar

10 9 8 7 6 5 4 3 2 1

Chronicle books and gifts are available at special quantity discounts to corporations, professional associations, literacy programs, and other organizations. For details and discount information, please contact our premiums department at corporatesales@chroniclebooks.com or at 1-800-759-0190.

CHRONICLE PRISM

Chronicle Prism is an imprint of Chronicle Books LLC,
680 Second Street, San Francisco, California 94107

www.chronicleprism.com

CONTENTS

INTRODUCTION

WELCOME!

Welcome to learning about your Human Design. I am so excited to share my greatest passion with you.

When I first discovered Human Design in 2017, I did what most people do—I ordered every Human Design book I could find. But it didn't take long to notice there was something missing. Where was the fun, practical, and aesthetically pleasing guide that made this system easy to understand and implement? There wasn't one. Little did I know then that Human Design would transform my life, and that I'd become one of the leading voices in this practice. Now I'm thrilled to bring you the very book I once wished existed.

I sense this book landed in your lap at the perfect time, just like Human Design did for me. Human Design finds you when you're ready for it. You're about to embark on a journey of self-discovery, energetic alignment, and manifestation of your dream life.

WHAT IS HUMAN DESIGN?

Before we dive in, let's take a moment to understand what Human Design is all about.

Human Design is a self-awareness system that helps you recognize how your energy works. It provides insights into your personality, your decision-making processes, and the ways you naturally interact with the world around you.

Think of it as a user manual for your life. Just as every device comes with instructions to use it effectively, Human Design gives you a guide to understanding your unique inner workings. It's a personalized blueprint for living your best life, highlighting your strengths and potential challenges, and choosing the most authentic path to navigate your journey.

By learning your Human Design, you'll gain clarity about your life's purpose, make decisions that truly feel right, and honor your energy in a way that brings fulfillment and authenticity. It's like having a custom road map to help you sail through life with greater ease and satisfaction.

WHERE DOES IT COME FROM?

Human Design originated in 1987 from the experiences of Ra Uru Hu, born Alan Robert Krakower, a teacher living on Ibiza. In January of that year, he encountered a brilliant, radiant light and the sound of "The Voice" that asked him, "Are you ready to work?" During an intense eight-day period that followed, Ra underwent a mystical encounter that introduced him to the foundational principles and imparted to him the "Design of Forms," or what we now call the Human Design System.

This encounter was deeply spiritual and transformative. Ra spent years meticulously studying, refining, and teaching Human Design, transforming it into a structured and accessible framework that people around the world could use to understand themselves and their energy.

At its essence, Human Design combines ancient wisdom with modern science. It brings together knowledge from systems that have been around for thousands of years, including astrology, the Chinese I Ching, the Kabbalah Tree of Life, and the Hindu chakra system. Each one adds a unique piece to the puzzle:

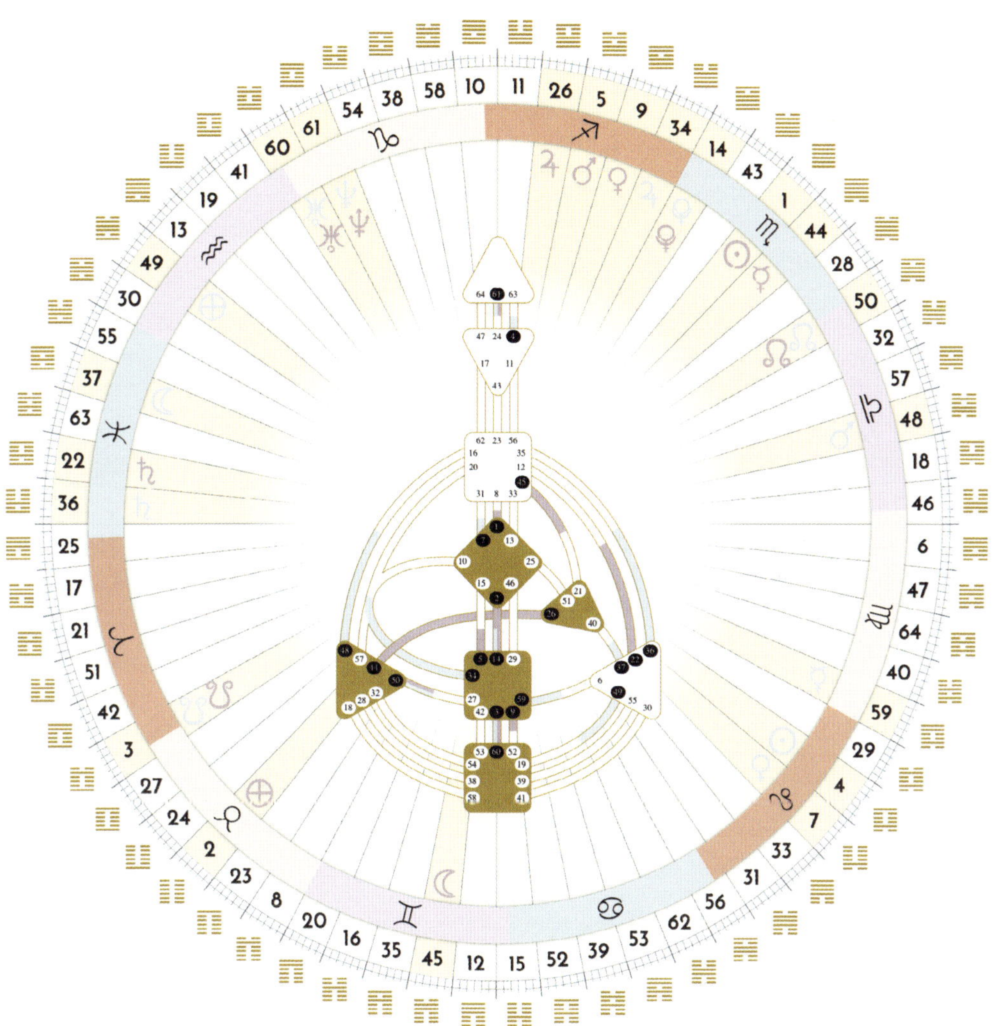
10 11 26 5 9 34 14 43 1 44 28 50 32 57 48 18 46 6 47 64 40 59 29 4 7 33 31 56 62 53 39 52 15 12 45 35 16 20 8 23 2 24 27 3 42 51 21 17 25 36 22 63 37 55 30 49 13 19 41 60 61 54 38 58

- Astrology shows how the positions of planets influence who we are.
- The I Ching, an ancient Chinese system, forms the foundation of Human Design, providing insights into our personality traits and life themes.
- The Kabbalah Tree of Life offers the structure for the BodyGraph, the chart used in Human Design, which maps how different aspects of ourselves are interconnected.
- The Hindu chakra system, which describes seven Energy Centers, is expanded upon in Human Design to help us understand our evolved nine Energy Centers.

Human Design also weaves in modern science to make this system even more comprehensive.

- Quantum physics explains how neutrinos, tiny particles of energy flowing through the universe, impact our lives and influence who we are.
- Genetics link the 64 Gates—our gifts—in Human Design to the 64 codons in human DNA, highlighting the connection between our energetic design and our biology.
- Biochemistry helps us understand how energy moves through our body, showing how our unique design affects the way we function and interact with the world.

Ra Uru Hu emphasized that Human Design is a system for the present and future, designed to help people navigate the challenges of modern life by understanding their energy and unique blueprint. After receiving this knowledge, Ra dedicated his life to teaching and refining Human Design. Over time, it has been widely adopted, evolving into a globally recognized tool for self-awareness, personal growth, and transformation.

I am deeply grateful for the ancient wisdom and cutting-edge science that contributed to Human Design's creation. This book is a testament to the endless insights these traditions provide, and I hope it inspires you to explore your own gifts and challenges in a meaningful way.

THE BENEFITS OF LEARNING HUMAN DESIGN

Perhaps you have experimented with a personality test, like Enneagram or Myers-Briggs (MBTI), and wondered how those systems actually impact your everyday life. Or maybe you got great results and an action plan, only to find out a year later that your personality type has changed. That's because most of the self-report questionnaires out there are subjective, based on your answers to a series of multiple-choice questions that you answer in one phase of your life. Who's to say you're even in the right headspace to take it?

Even astrology, which I truly love, can sometimes feel impractical. For example, how do I really know what to do with the fact that my Uranus is in Capricorn in the seventh house? While I'm always looking for ways to interpret astrology in my own life, it doesn't always offer clear, actionable guidance for the micro moments of our everyday decision-making.

That's where Human Design shines. It's not just another personality profiling tool—it's an actionable system you can use every single day, with every decision. It gives you a practical road map to navigate your life in alignment with your true self.

In my humble opinion, Human Design is one of the best tools out there. It's a culmination of so many other systems to give you a rich, layered perspective on your energy, purpose, and potential. It takes the guesswork out of life and is all-encompassing.

Learning and applying Human Design can be life-changing, especially if you feel stuck or unfulfilled in your career, relationships, or personal life. Whether you're exploring self-discovery, seeking clarity on your life's purpose, or navigating a major life transition, Human Design offers personalized insights to help you find alignment and fulfillment.

Here are a few ways Human Design can support you:

- You feel stuck or stagnant in your life, career, or relationships.
- You're seeking a deeper understanding of yourself and your life's purpose.
- You have a major transition or decision ahead.
- You want to optimize your habits to work with your energy, not against it.
- You often experience frustration, bitterness, anger, or disappointment.
- You desire a deeper understanding of your partner or loved ones.
- You want to manifest your desires more quickly and effectively.

Human Design gives you a way to understand your soul, mind, body, and emotions. It offers a deeper understanding of how you operate, providing clarity on questions like: Are you an emotional being or not? Do you have a strong sense of direction? By the end of this book, you'll have answers to these questions and much more.

This system also gives you permission to embrace your uniqueness. Instead of feeling pressure to fit into societal expectations, Human Design helps you fully own and express what makes you different. It's an invitation to confidently live as your authentic self.

Most importantly, Human Design empowers you to reach your highest potential. By aligning with your unique energy blueprint, you can step into exactly who you are meant to be and unlock the fullness of your life's purpose.

THINGS TO KNOW BEFORE WE START . . .

When it comes to spiritual modalities like Human Design, one common question is: "Does it predict my future?" The answer is no—Human Design isn't predictive.

Human Design is a tool. There is nothing to believe in; it simply requires experimenting and observing how your design shows up in your life. It's a guide to help you make meaningful changes and start living in alignment with your dreams, values, and purpose. There are no strict rules—just suggestions to help you discover what truly works for you in real life.

Before we begin, I want to mention that Human Design can feel overwhelming at first, and that's okay. My goal is to make the Human Design process simple, practical, and easy to apply.

You'll notice throughout this book that I sometimes reference more than one name for some aspects of Human Design. For example, when learning about Authority, you'll also see "Sacral Authority" as "Gut Feelings." My intention is to present you with the most everyday language, or other interpretations that may exist beyond my own, while honoring the original language from Ra Uru Hu.

I'd like to point out here that working with Human Design is a journey, not a destination. Engaging with this system isn't about learning it once and then suddenly finding yourself living your most aligned life. It's an ongoing journey that involves continually learning about your chart, integrating this knowledge into your daily life, and making decisions that resonate with your unique design. This process also includes revisiting the tool regularly to remind yourself of who you truly are and to reinforce your understanding. You never fully "arrive"; rather, you continuously evolve and embody your true self through this transformative journey. Embrace each step, each revelation, as a part of a lifelong exploration into your deepest self.

HOW TO USE THIS BOOK

Inside this book, you'll find Human Design explained in the most grounded, practical, and easy-to-implement way possible. I've included reflection questions, daily practices, and tools to help you start living your design. I hope you love it!

You'll start by looking up your Human Design chart and filling out the blank BodyGraph template provided on page 33. Then we'll break down each part of your chart step by step with prompts to help you explore and reflect on your design.

We'll delve into how to use this information to make aligned decisions, explore tools for manifesting your dream life, and look at how Human Design can lead to finding your true life's purpose.

MY JOURNEY

Before I guide you through your Human Design journey, let me share a bit about my own. It will give you a taste of how Human Design works and get you comfortable with some of the terms we'll be using throughout the book.

It started at 11:30 p.m. in bed one night, scrolling through images on my phone, watching everyone else live their dream life when I should have been sleeping—a familiar routine. I was twenty-three and in my first apartment after college. It was my entry into corporate America and adulthood, and I had just gone through a life-altering breakup. I was living back in my hometown while all my college friends seemed to be experiencing exciting new cities post-graduation. I was about a year into my big-girl job at a big Fortune 500 company—a gig that locals were impressed by—but I was beginning to experience some existential dread. Is this the rest of my life? I wondered. Is this it? Do I just wake up every day, go to the job I'm okay at, and work hard for something I don't care about or have a single ounce of passion for? Is this all my life has to offer?

I knew the answer to that last question was no. I felt it in my gut. And it wasn't anything short of panic-inducing to have this realization. But nights like these continued. Every day looked like waking up at the last possible second, rushing out the door, and playing a fake, more enthusiastic version of myself all day, in and out of meetings about unreachable deadlines, corporate power trips, and big egos. Then I'd come home exhausted, try to get a workout in, make dinner, and go to bed to return to my doomscrolling.

I knew I was meant for more, and there were physical signs, too. My body felt tight, and my stomach hurt constantly. I knew I was meant to live a fuller life but had zero clue what that actually meant, how it would happen, or what it would even look like.

So I picked up a pen and started writing down my dreams. This became my nightly ritual and my first real step toward manifestation. I turned my doomscrolling into inspiration, using it to clue myself into what I deeply desired. When I saw my sorority sister quit corporate life to start her own company, I now chose not to feel jealous, ashamed, or sad. Instead, I saw it as proof that bigger things were possible for me, too.

I was so ready to feel satisfied in my own life, and I often wrote about dreams like these:

- I want to help people.
- I want to deepen my spirituality.
- I want to work in wellness.
- I want to be financially free.
- I want to share my unique way of living.
- I want to live in California.

- I want to be in a healthy, happy, soulful relationship.
- I want to access my creativity.

For much of the duration of this nightly ritual, the dream life I envisioned seemed so out of reach. I had developed a clear picture of what I wanted, but my reality didn't match up.

I was stuck, creatively drained, unsure how I could genuinely help people. Then one evening, Human Design found me. Before I knew it, I had booked a Human Design reading, scoured the internet, and bought every Human Design book I could find. At first my plan was to dive in just for fun. Little did I know this would be the start of the transformative realignment I so desperately needed.

Here's how Human Design unfolded for me. First I learned my Energy Type: I'm a Generator. I'm designed to be full of life, sharing my warm energy with the world by doing work I love, not by feeling drained and depleted every day, stuck in work that didn't light me up, as I was at the time.

Next, I learned how to work with my Energy Type using something called Strategy. As a Generator, my Strategy is to Wait to Respond to the opportunities that naturally show up instead of chasing or forcing things to happen. Up until then I had been chasing and forcing a life I wanted so badly—and getting nowhere.

I discovered how to make intuitive decisions using something called Authority. Mine is Sacral Authority, which means I'm guided by my Gut Feelings. Suddenly, the gut-wrenching tightness I'd been feeling in my body made sense—it was my body and my intuition trying to speak to me. Even my constant stomachaches finally had an explanation. I was unhappy and hadn't made the right choices for myself.

I also learned that we each have two sides to our personality, and aligning with both helps us stay on our path and live out our purpose.

This is known as Profile. My Profile (5/1) is all about helping others and sharing solutions while balancing my need to investigate everything and set boundaries to manage others' expectations. I'd always found myself diving into endless rabbit holes of research, sharing everything I learned in hopes of helping others. Now I understood that this was a core part of my personality and how I'm designed to live on purpose.

I also discovered that when I'm in alignment (we'll talk about that later in the book), I feel joy and satisfaction, which make up my Signature Theme in Human Design. And when I'm out of alignment, I feel frustrated and stuck, which is my Not-Self Theme. Boy, was I ever so living in misalignment. I was filled with frustration day in and day out. Joy and satisfaction were foreign to me.

I learned about the energies I'm receptive or vulnerable to from other people, and where I carry energy and impact others through my Energy Centers. For example, I discovered I feel the emotional weather from others and impact people with my willpower. This made sense, as I've always felt affected by what other people experience emotionally, and I've always had a natural way of uplifting people and empowering them. I just didn't know these were so innate to me or how to work with them.

Through my Definition in Human Design, I discovered that I'm designed to collaborate with others and process information in the company of people, rather than trying to do everything on my own. This clicked immediately—I'm always more productive when others are nearby. Yet, at the time, I was spending so much energy trying to make my dreams a reality completely on my own.

I learned that I have twenty-six unique gifts, called Gates, in my Human Design chart. My most prominent gift is divine creativity, and this explained why I've always felt a deep desire to tap into my creative side, a thread that showed up repeatedly in my journaling over the years. It also explained my constant need to write and express myself—it's part of my design.

I found out one of my core gifts, through something called a Channel, is to be a visionary and follow my own unique direction and path in life. And that one of my greatest lessons with this is to take the leap because of how it inspires others. No wonder I had nudges to take a chance on myself; it was a part of my core gift in life to do so.

I discovered that I'm designed to do things differently and go against the status quo—this is quite literally the theme of my life and why I'm here. This theme is revealed through the Incarnation Cross, a part of Human Design that highlights our life's purpose on an energetic level. I'd always felt a natural pull to go left when everyone else was going right, or to follow my own path, even when it defied expectations. Now I understood that this is exactly how I'm designed to operate. My Incarnation Cross is the Left Angle Cross of Defiance, and it's become one of my favorite aspects of my Human Design.

It even uncovered how my body best digests food through my Digestion, an intricate part of our design that reveals how we can best nourish ourselves. For me, it's quite humorous, because mine revolves around being somewhat particular with food selections. If you know me, I am definitely not picky, but I am very particular about ingredients and the quality of food.

Another cool, eerily accurate piece was learning my Strongest Sense, which revealed to me that I'm born with uncanny Feelings that can just sense things. I have always been the person who says, "I just have a feeling" with zero context.

I learned that the Environments I thrive in are Valleys, which is symbolic of places where you can make connections and feel in touch with the world. This reminded me of my college years and how I thrived living in a place where I knew all my neighbors, could bump into my friends walking to class, and was right by the commotion of what was happening in town.

I also discovered how my brain sees the world through my View. This helped me with my manifesting practice, as it indicated that I tend to zoom in on things and get quite detailed. I started implementing this, and it kicked my manifestations into high gear.

Lastly, I discovered that Hope is the way my mind is motivated. So when I'm in conversation, my brain immediately processes things to look for the positive outcome or potential. I always knew I was a "hope-core" type of girl, but this confirmed it.

As you can imagine, I felt seen and validated in ways I so badly needed, but at the same time, I also felt confronted. This was a wake-up call to realizing the potential inside of me.

Human Design didn't need to convince me of anything—it simply showed me who I was. It felt eerily accurate, like holding a mirror to the highest version of myself. I knew, without a doubt, that this was my truth and that it was up to me to step into my fullest potential. I decided to experiment with it—after all, what did I have to lose? The life I already hated for a better one?

And so the journey began . . .

Now I'm writing this book from my home office in California, where I live with the love of my life. I'm surrounded by inspiring dreamers and doers. I've taught Human Design to thousands of people and share my wellness and spiritual wisdom with others daily. I get to be creative, and the more I embrace that, the more abundance flows into my life. Today I'm living my most aligned life—a reality I manifested by working with my Human Design. What once seemed like just a fun personality test turned out to unlock the version of myself I'd always dreamed of becoming.

"I often say Human Design is who you are before the world told you what to be."

CHAPTER 1

The FOUNDA-TIONS *of* HUMAN DESIGN

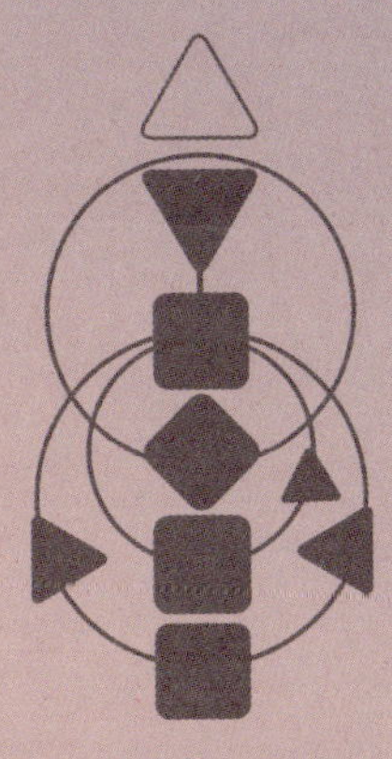

We're going to kick things off by learning the foundations of Human Design and how to read your Human Design chart (don't panic—it's not as complex as it looks!). I'll have you fill out your own Human Design chart details so that you can easily reference them throughout this book. Once we cover the foundations, I'll guide you through each part of your own Human Design step by step.

But before we look at your chart, let's look at a few terms and ideas that are essential to Human Design.

DECONDITIONING

Deconditioning is one of the focal points of Human Design and is crucial to understand as you learn about your chart and start this journey. So what is it?

Conditioning refers to how the energy and expectations from the world around us can influence us to stray from our true selves. Often it involves picking up habits and beliefs that don't really fit who we are deep down, based on what others expect or the social norms we encounter. This can come from family, friends, society, or any external influences that shape how we think, feel, and act.

Deconditioning, on the other hand, peels back those layers that aren't really you. It's like returning to your authentic self by shedding those external influences. This process involves getting to know your own Human Design chart deeply and starting to live in alignment with your true nature—whether that's how you best make decisions, how you use your energy, or where you might be vulnerable to outside pressures. This allows you to move from who you've been told you should be to who you actually are.

I often say Human Design is who you are before the world told you what to be.

ALIGNMENT

Alignment is when your actions, intentions, and energy are fully in sync with your values, dreams, and purpose. It's that feeling of being on the right path, where everything in your life—your relationships, career, health, and passions—feel connected, flowing, and meaningful. Instead of pushing or forcing things to happen, you're allowing life to unfold in a way that feels natural and deeply fulfilling. We'll talk a lot about alignment in this book, as it is one of the main goals of Human Design.

I like to think of alignment as driving on a long, beautiful road that's perfectly paved for you. Along the way, you see everything you love—your friends, your family, your hobbies, your passions. Your wildest dreams are just up ahead, coming straight toward you, and all you have to do is keep driving. There's no need to fight traffic or take detours. The road is clear because you're on the right path, and everything you've been dreaming of is already lined up, waiting for you to receive it.

Alignment happens when you stop trying to control the "how" and start trusting the flow of your energy. It's not about doing more or being someone you're not, but rather about moving through life in a way that honors your unique strengths, desires, and design.

But here's the truth: For most of us, alignment doesn't just happen. It requires clarity and self-awareness. It requires understanding what's uniquely you—your natural way of making decisions, your energy flow, and what truly lights you up.

The journey to alignment begins with tuning in to yourself and stepping away from the noise of what you "should" be doing. It's about uncovering your unique path and walking it with confidence and trust. Alignment is where your power lies, and it's where your dream life begins.

MANIFESTATION

Now let's talk about one of the keys to creating your dream life: manifestation.

When you first hear the word "manifestation," it might sound a little woo-woo or like something out of a mystical practice (and sure, it can be). But at its core, manifestation is incredibly simple—it's the act of bringing your desires into reality. It's the process of turning your dreams, hopes, and visions into something tangible.

Think of manifestation as the bridge between what you imagine and what you experience. It's taking something you desire—whether it's a feeling, a relationship, a career, or even a material possession—and drawing it into your life.

Perhaps you see someone living a life you'd like to live. Maybe it's their situation you admire, like the city they live in, the job they have, and the relationships they have. Maybe it's the more material things you admire, like their clothes, their car, or their home. Maybe it's their personality and the way they hold themselves, speak, and share their light.

Or perhaps it's not about a specific person but a culmination of people, situations, experiences, and material things you want to call in. It's more about how you want to feel. Whatever or whoever it may be, we all have hopes, dreams, visions, and goals. We all have things we want to happen in our lives. We all want to manifest.

Now why am I bringing up manifestation in a book about Human Design? Because, in my experience, *Human Design is one of the most powerful manifestation tools in existence.*

Here's why: Manifestation works best when you're in alignment with your energy and your highest self. When you start living in a way that honors your unique design, everything begins to flow. You stop chasing your dreams and start attracting them. You create a magnetism that draws your wildest visions toward you.

In the world of manifestation, there are countless techniques—visualizations, affirmations, scripting, and more. But what if you could harness a manifestation process that's tailored specifically to you? That's exactly what Human Design offers: a personalized map of your energy that shows you how to align with your natural flow, make decisions that feel right, and embody the version of yourself that effortlessly attracts what you desire.

WHAT IS A HUMAN DESIGN CHART?

Your Human Design Chart, also called a BodyGraph, is created using your birth information—specifically, the time, date, and location of your birth. This information helps us figure out the planetary positions right at the moment you were born. This part of your chart reveals your personality, or conscious side of your chart, showing you how you see yourself and highlighting your unique traits, strengths, and challenges.

Human Design also looks at the planetary positions about eighty-eight days before you were born. According to Human Design, this is said to be when your soul enters your body while you're still in your mother's womb. This phase forms the unconscious, or design, part of your chart. It reflects those deeper patterns that shape how you automatically respond to the world around you. While the conscious side of your chart shows how you interact with the world on a day-to-day level, the unconscious side reveals your deeper tendencies—often driving your behaviors in ways you don't realize.

Why is having the exact time of your birth important? Think of it like capturing a snapshot of the celestial vibes that were in play when you came into this world. Each minute can change the positions of the planets and the way your chart is formed, which is why nailing down your exact birth time is key to truly understanding your unique energy.

If you don't have that exact time, don't worry! Know that even without the precise minute, lots of the important parts of your chart remain consistent throughout the day of your birth. You can try estimating if you have a rough idea of when you were born, like "after dinner" or "early in the morning." However, below are some ideas to try and find your birth time:

- Ask your parents or family members if they have any documentation, such as a baby book, old photos or videos with timestamps, or even a diary.
- Contact the hospital where you were born. They may have records that include your exact birth time.
- Consult an astrologer who specializes in chart rectification. This is someone skilled at astrological timing that can analyze significant life events based on transits.
- Use a spiritual tool called a pendulum to ask yes/no questions about your birth time.
- Check local newspapers around your birth date. Sometimes, they publish birth announcements that include the time of birth.

There are a lot of online software and apps to generate your Human Design Chart. I'm a bit biased, but I love ours the most (see page 261); however, all of them are good and will get you what you need. There's an option to download your chart as a PDF, and I recommend doing that and printing it out! It's just one page.

Your BodyGraph is a map that lays out your strengths, challenges, and how you can navigate life. By tapping into the insights from your

BodyGraph, you'll have a powerful guide to help you make decisions, connect with others, and live your best, most authentic life.

As I've mentioned, it may feel a bit complicated in the beginning, but I'm here to make it easy for you.

Human Design Chart Components

Once you have your Human Design Chart, you'll see different components that together create a unique picture of how you are designed to navigate life, interact with others, and express your gifts. Let's get comfortable with these components:

Your *BodyGraph* is another way to refer to your Human Design Chart. This is the graph of energy within your body. Often, we call this your energetic blueprint, but we'll stick to Human Design Chart.

Your *Energy Type* describes how your energy functions and is the foundation of your Human Design. It reveals how you naturally interact with the world, helps you understand your unique rhythm, and shows you how to engage with life in a way that feels effortless and aligned.

You use your *Strategy* to bring in aligned opportunities based on your Energy Type. Following your Strategy helps you avoid resistance and friction, and allows for life to flow in a more synchronistic and fulfilling way.

Your *Authority* is a powerful mechanism. It's your inner compass that guides you to make decisions that are deeply aligned with your true self. It's what you lean on to help you cut through noise and external pressure to make choices that feel right for you. Essentially, Authority is your intuition.

Your *Profile* reveals the two primary sides of your personality: how you view yourself and how others perceive you. It's a key to understanding your role in life and helps you live in harmony with your purpose, calling, or life theme.

Your *Signature Theme* is the feeling that awakens inside you when you are in alignment, or as we like to say in Human Design, you're living your design. It's the signpost that shows you're on the right track and aligned with your true purpose.

Your *Not-Self Theme* is the feeling that signals when you've veered off your authentic path. It's a sign of resistance, blockage, and misalignment with your energy. It's an opportunity to reflect, course-correct, and realign with your design.

Energy Centers are the shapes, or energy hubs, within our BodyGraph that reveal where we're receptive to energy from others or where we transmit energy outward. Each Energy Center offers insights into how you make an impact, how you are vulnerable, and what lessons you can learn.

Your *Definition* shows how your energy flows and interacts with others, giving you insight into how you may work well with others, such as whether you're more self-sufficient or need collaboration. Your Definition also shows how you might process things energetically, whether you move through things quickly, need to move energy and information through your body, or take a detached approach before fully processing. Your Definition influences your sense of independence, how you form relationships, and where you might seek connection.

Gates represent the specific gifts and potential you carry, and how these traits can express themselves, depending on circumstances and other influences.

Channels are the pathways that connect your Gates and reflect your core strengths and consistent, impactful gifts. They provide a deeper understanding of how your gifts work together to shape your energy and purpose.

Your *Incarnation Cross* reflects the overarching theme of your life, guiding your purpose and energetic contribution to the world. It's the story you're here to live and the unique calling you're meant to express through your gifts.

Your *Digestion*, formally called your Determination, is the optimal way your body is designed to process both food and information. Following your Digestion aligns your body for greater clarity, energy, and well-being.

Your *Strongest Sense*, formally called Cognition, is like your superpower—it's the way you best tune in to the world. It acts as a guide to help you determine what feels good and aligned in your life. Honoring your Strongest Sense allows you to sharpen your intuitive awareness and connect more deeply to your surroundings.

Your *Environment* is all about the spaces where you feel most comfortable, inspired, and aligned. It encompasses not just physical locations but the qualities of those places. Being in the right environment reduces resistance and supports your energy flow, helping you feel more balanced.

Your *View* reveals the lens through which you naturally view the world, particularly whether you zoom in on the details or take a wide-angle view. Staying true to your perspective allows you to see things clearly. It's less about what you look at and more about how you look at it.

Your *Motivation* reveals how your mind is motivated to understand things, the unique force that drives your perspective and inspires your thoughts and actions. It shapes how you engage with life and process the world. When you're aligned with your Motivation, your mind feels clear, focused, and naturally directed.

Reading a Human Design Chart

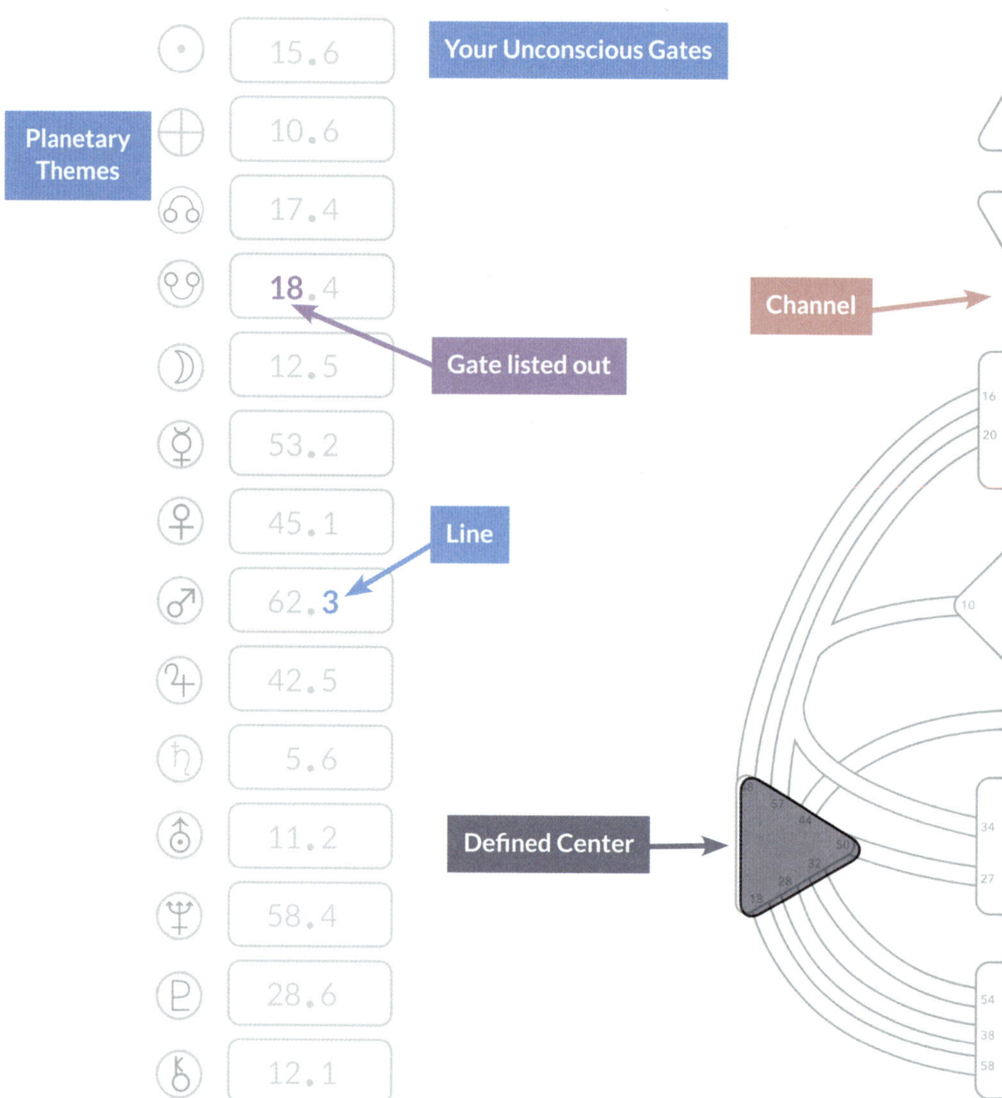

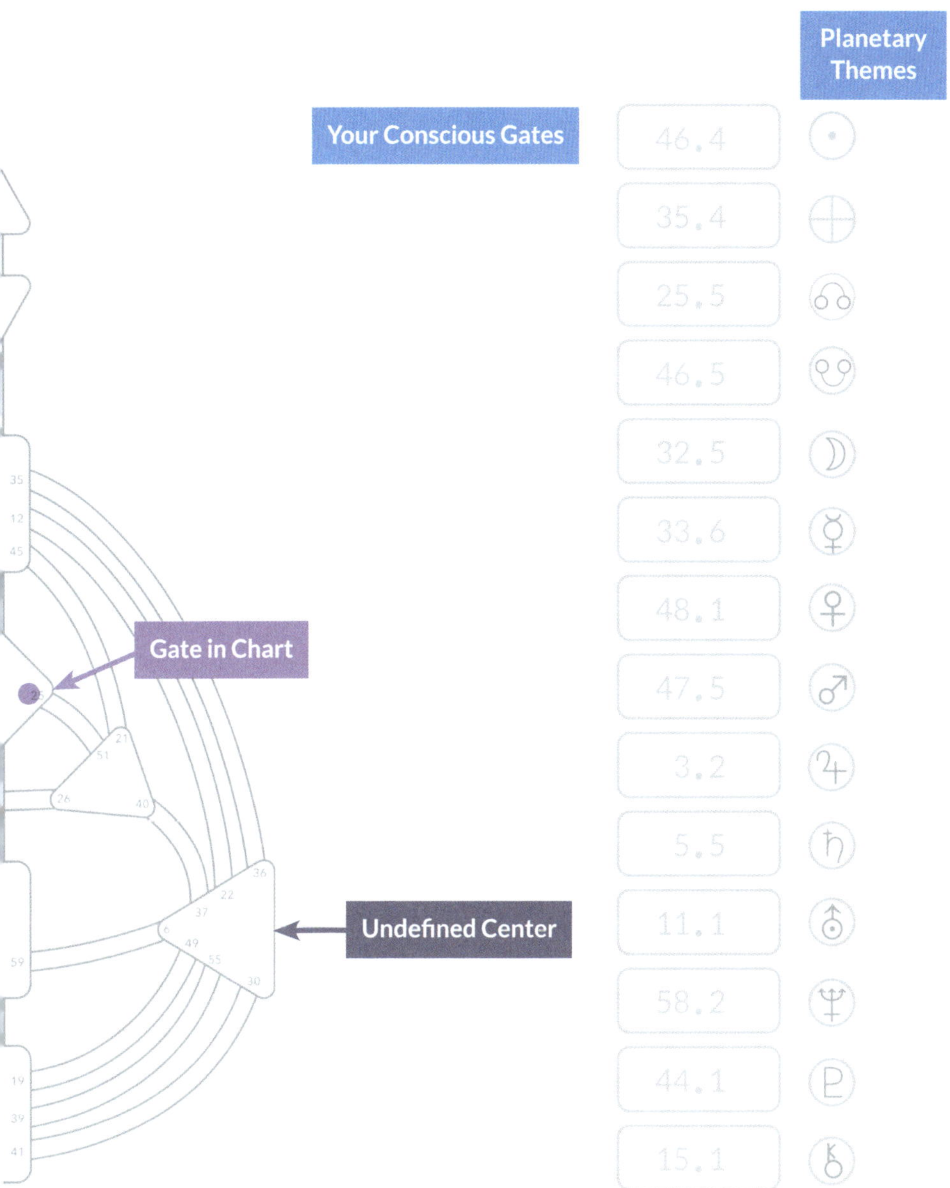
Planetary Themes
Your Conscious Gates
46.4
35.4
25.5
46.5
32.5
33.6
48.1
47.5
3.2
5.5
11.1
58.2
44.1
15.1
Gate in Chart
Undefined Center
35
12
45
25
21
51
26
40
36
22
37
6
49
55
30
59
19
39
41

Your Human Design Chart

To look up your Human Design Chart, go to www.thedesignofyou.com or head to page 261 and scan the QR code.

MY ENERGY TYPE ______________________________

MY STRATEGY ______________________________

MY AUTHORITY ______________________________

MY SIGNATURE THEME ______________________________

MY NOT-SELF THEME ______________________________

MY PROFILE ______________________________

MY DEFINED CENTERS* ______________________________

MY UNDEFINED CENTERS* ______________________________

MY DEFINITION ______________________________

MY INCARNATION CROSS ______________________________

MY CHANNELS** ______________________________

MY GATES ______________________________

MY DIGESTION ______________________________

MY STRONGEST SENSE ______________________________

MY ENVIRONMENT ______________________________

MY VIEW ______________________________

MY MOTIVATION ______________________________

* *See page 131 for help determining these.*

** *If you're a Reflector, you won't have any Channels; see page 186 (chapter 8) for more details.*

In the blank BodyGraph below, color in your chart and fill out as many of the numbers as you can.

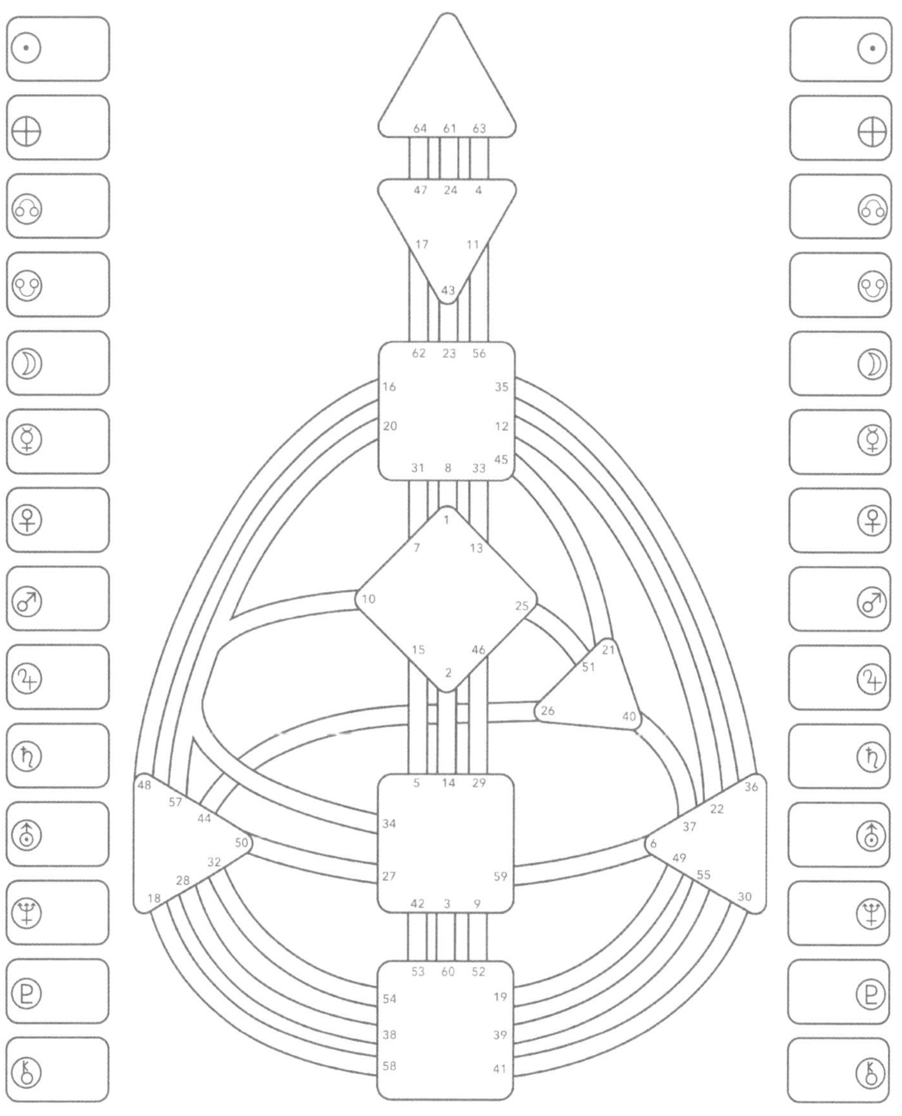

"Understanding your Energy Type shows you how to align with your natural rhythms, avoid burnout, and navigate life in a way that feels purposeful and easeful."

CHAPTER 2

HARNESSING *Your* ENERGY

Now we're ready to dive into what we call The Big Three in Human Design. If you are familiar with astrology (and most people are—I call it the gateway drug to Human Design!), you may know the most important elements of your astrological chart are your sun sign, moon sign, and rising/ascending sign—a.k.a. The Big Three. In Human Design, there is also a Big Three: your Energy Type, Authority, and Profile. So while in astrology I'm a Scorpio sun, Gemini moon, and Cancer rising, in Human Design I'm a 5/1 Sacral Generator.

In the next few chapters, we'll dig into each of The Big Three to learn more about your own unique Human Design.

YOUR ENERGY TYPE

We begin with your Energy Type. This is the most fundamental aspect of your Human Design Chart. It explains how the energy in your body interacts with the world around you so you can best utilize it in various parts of your life, including in relationships and at work.

Understanding your Energy Type shows you how to align with your natural rhythms, avoid burnout, and navigate life in a way that feels purposeful and easeful. Whether it's in your relationships, career, or personal growth, knowing your Energy Type is the first step to unlocking alignment.

There are five Energy Types: Manifestors, Generators, Manifesting Generators, Projectors, and Reflectors.

What is your Energy Type? Fill it in below.

MY ENERGY TYPE IS ______________________________

When learning about each Energy Type, you'll explore . . .

ROLE
The unique way your Energy Type contributes to the world and interacts with others

ENERGETIC GIFT
The natural gift or value you bring when you're living in alignment

STRATEGY
The specific approach you're designed to use to create flow and ease in life

ALIGNMENT THEMES
Signposts that show when you're on or off track

POPULATION
How common or rare your Energy Type is globally

ALIGNMENT TIP
A practical takeaway to help you thrive in your Energy Type

AURA
The energetic field around you that influences how others perceive and experience your Energy Type

BIGGEST LESSON
The key challenge you're here to grow through

FAMOUS MANIFESTORS
Fun examples of well-known figures who share your Energy Type

We'll unpack what makes each Energy Type unique, how you can lean in to your natural energy, and practical tips. Think of it as your personal cheat sheet for working with your energy.

Understanding the Energy Types

Here's a quick snapshot of the five Energy Types before we do a deep dive on each.

MANIFESTORS, as the fire starters, initiate things. They get the ball rolling on new ideas or big changes by acting on their inner push. They're like the spark that lights the fire. It's their job to tell everyone what they're thinking, which gets everyone pumped and ready to jump in. While they naturally inspire action in others, their role as initiators stands strong on its own.

GENERATORS, as the life force, are the builders or doers. With their enduring and robust energy, Generators take ideas and give them life. They keep the wheels turning, making sure everything that was started actually gets finished, and they do it with sparkly warm energy.

MANIFESTING GENERATORS, as the multi-passionate powerhouses, take all that solid groundwork and kick it up a notch. They move fast, juggling different parts of the project and pushing boundaries. They're the ones who bring fresh ideas and quick fixes into the mix, making everything more effective and fun.

PROJECTORS, as the guides, have the bird's-eye view. They see how everything works together and guide others with their insights. They make sure the Generators and Manifesting Generators are putting their energy in the right places, helping everything run smoother and smarter.

REFLECTORS, as the mirrors, show everyone the big picture. They help people see what's working and what's not, which can be a game changer. Their ability to reflect the state of their environment makes their feedback and insight crucial, whether in group settings or as consultants who observe and advise on organizational health. They ensure that practices are aligned with core values and adapt to necessary changes.

Manifestors

The Fire Starters

ROLE OF MANIFESTORS

Manifestors are the fire starters and trailblazers! They create momentum, start movements, shake things up, and initiate newness. They are born with strong voices and the energy to be different, express themselves, and do things their own way. Their role is to take their divine ideas and share them with the world so they can use their gifts (based on their own Energy Type) to make them happen. They're quite literally here to get the party started (energetically speaking). For example, a Manifestor is the one who gets a burst of energy, or an impulse, for an idea, and if the idea is in alignment with them, shares it with the rest of us. They're incredibly inspiring and are meant to bring new projects to the world.

THE GIFT MANIFESTORS BRING TO THE WORLD

Their gift is to light a fire in everyone else and hopefully inspire them to get involved in their plans. I often describe Manifestors as bus drivers. They get big ideas out of nowhere and are here to get everyone on board.

MANIFESTOR STRATEGY: INFORM THEN INITIATE

The way Manifestors best work with their energy is by what we call "Informing Then Initiating." Basically, Manifestors are here to start things—they get these bold ideas or bursts of inspiration, and they're designed to just go for them (manifest them)! But here's the key: Before

ROLE
The Initiator

ENERGETIC GIFT
To bring new ideas and ways of doing things to the world

STRATEGY
Inform then initiate

ALIGNMENT THEMES
Peace and anger

POPULATION
~9 percent

ALIGNMENT TIP
Let people in on your plans and don't stay small

AURA
Big and protective

BIGGEST LESSON
Learn to inform and become unapologetically bold

FAMOUS MANIFESTORS
Johnny Depp, Gloria Steinem, Maya Angelou, Martha Stewart, Adele

jumping into action or initiating, they need to inform the people who might be affected by what they're about to do.

So why is informing so important? Think of it like giving a friendly heads-up. Manifestors naturally have big, impactful energy that can sometimes catch people off guard. Informing lets others know what's coming, so there's less resistance. It's not about asking for permission (remember—Manifestors don't need anyone's approval!). It's just about saying, "Hey, here's what I'm planning," to keep things flowing smoothly. That way, when they go to initiate there's no confusion.

For example, if a Manifestor decides they're going to rearrange the furniture in the living room, they'd let their family know first instead of just surprising everyone.

Another example: A Manifestor at work may have a super-innovative project idea. Aware of their Strategy, they are sure to share their vision with their team and supervisors first, explaining the concept, potential impact, and the steps they plan to take to make it happen first.

These simple acts of informing allow for the Manifestors to move forward with their plans more peacefully.

And then once they've informed, Manifestors are free to initiate and make things happen. They don't need to wait for anyone's go-ahead; their job is to bring new ideas and energy into the world. Informing might feel awkward at first, but it's the secret sauce that helps Manifestors use their powerful energy without creating friction. It's all about acting with ease and alignment!

MANIFESTATION TIP FOR MANIFESTOR'S STRATEGY

Inform others about what you're doing, not to ask for their approval, but to clear the path and reduce resistance. Trust your inner urges and act on them boldly. When you embrace your role as a trailblazer, the universe aligns to support your vision.

THE MANIFESTOR AURA: BIG AND PROTECTIVE

When a Manifestor walks into a room you can feel it, but just because you can feel it, doesn't mean you'll like it. Formally, a Manifestor's aura is described as Repelling, which means it can repel people just as much as it can catch their attention. People are either drawn to Manifestors or taken aback. I like to reframe this to the word "protective," because although it sounds harsh to have a "repelling aura" it's quite protective in nature, acting as a natural filter and allowing only those who truly connect with the Manifestor's energy and intentions to stay close. This protective mechanism saves the Manifestor's energy and keeps them surrounded by people who genuinely understand and support their journey. A Manifestor is designed to be bold and have a great deal of confidence, and people either

Tips for Informing as Manifestors

INFORMING IS	INFORMING IS NOT
Communicating something you have happening in your life	*Asking for permission from others*
Giving people information about what you are doing	*Signing up to be misunderstood or controlled*
Telling others what you are thinking	*Waiting for things to happen to you*
Letting people in on your ideas	*Justifying your decisions by sharing with others*
Announcing your plans	*Assuming people know something when you didn't communicate it*
Disclosing necessary info to the right people	*Giving away all your ideas*
Alerting those impacted	*Telling everyone your plans (beyond those impacted)*

love it or hate it, but it's this beautiful natural sifting process that allows Manifestors to find their people easily. There are no guessing games for the Manifestors—they'll know when someone is for them or not. Going back to the bus analogy—Manifestors don't need to convince people to come on to their bus—the ones who want to join in on their plans will. How lovely is that?

LESSONS AND DECONDITIONING TIPS FOR MANIFESTORS

Although designed to kick-start things, be bold, and have a big aura, Manifestors often struggle with these traits as they move through life. You sometimes feel you are "too much" and can't go the way you want to. You may feel like your ideas are too big or too daring. Your lesson is to become unapologetically yourself and not let other people make you feel small. There is no such thing as shining too bright. You're the fire starters, after all; you're meant to ignite something in all of us.

Leaning in to rest is another lesson for you as a Manifestor. Although you are trailblazers, you are not designed with consistent fuel to go, go, go. You must give yourselves rest. This is how more of your big ideas come to you. Manifestors may feel pressured to be "on" 24/7, but this is just conditioning. Your biggest flex is taking a break between initiating and waiting for something new to emerge over time.

Another key lesson is that informing isn't asking for permission. Often, you may have had experiences where you've told someone your ideas, and others disagreed with you. This causes you to feel small (against your nature) and not want to disclose your plans to others. This is a massive form of conditioning for the Manifestor and can create friction within yourself. A big lesson for you to learn is that informing is simply letting others know so that they can either join in on your plans or step aside so that you can keep firing away.

MANIFESTORS AT WORK

Manifestors excel when they can work independently and on their own terms. They are great at starting new projects and often lead the way. They need a job where they can be in charge of what they do and when they do it. Manifestors work well when they can have busy times followed by quiet times to rest and think of new ideas. It's important for them to communicate openly with their coworkers to keep everything running smoothly. They thrive in roles where they can innovate and are not bound by too many rules or restrictions.

MANIFESTORS IN RELATIONSHIPS

Manifestors bring a special energy to their relationships and need partners who respect their independence and unique nature. The ideal partner for a Manifestor is someone who trusts them deeply, embraces their powerful energy, and does not try to slow them down or control them. This partner should encourage the Manifestor's spontaneity and creativity, allowing them to express themselves fully. Manifestors appreciate being with someone who understands their need for freedom and supports their endeavors without needing constant reassurance or agreement.

MANIFESTATION TIP FOR MANIFESTORS

Destroy the idea that you're too much or too brave. Embrace your natural ability to initiate and inspire. Your power lies in starting things and setting them into motion—not necessarily in finishing them. Allow yourself to act on your creative bursts of energy without guilt. You are designed to bring about transformation and change, so step into your role with confidence and let your unique energy light the path for others.

Generators

The Life Force

ROLE OF GENERATORS

Generators are the life force of the world, born with an abundance of energy that can last all day if focused on the right things. They are natural doers who uplift everyone around them by engaging in activities they truly love. Their magnetic and warm aura feels like a big embrace, wrapping around people and making them feel energized.

THE GIFT GENERATORS BRING TO THE WORLD

Generators have the gift of creating and lifting up the energy of everyone around them. When they do things that light them up from the inside, their energy spills out, benefiting everyone. This makes it vital for Generators to choose activities that truly excite them, as their happiness and energy contribute significantly to the world's positivity.

GENERATOR STRATEGY: WAIT TO RESPOND

Generators have a unique approach to navigating life, primarily guided by the Strategy of "Waiting to Respond." This means engaging with the world as it comes to them, rather than pushing to make things happen. Generators are like magnets, drawing opportunities toward them effortlessly. Their job is to wait for something to show up in their world—an idea, a text message, a question, a person, or even just a feeling—and then respond to it. That's when the magic happens!

ROLE
The Life Force

ENERGETIC GIFT
To create and lift up the energy of the world

STRATEGY
Wait to respond

ALIGNMENT THEMES
Satisfaction and frustration

POPULATION
~36 percent

ALIGNMENT TIP
Follow what lights you up and trust your gut

AURA
Open and enveloping

BIGGEST LESSON
Learn to say no and prioritize your own satisfaction

FAMOUS GENERATORS
Beyoncé, Oprah Winfrey, Albert Einstein, Dolly Parton, LeBron James

But what does "respond" mean? It means listening to your gut. Generators have this incredible built-in guide—their gut feeling—that tells them whether something is a yes or a no. If it's a yes, they'll feel excited, open, or energized. If it's a no, they'll feel heavy, closed off, or drained. Their body literally knows what's right for them, and all they have to do is trust it.

For example, let's say a Generator wants to plan a vacation. Instead of picking a destination out of nowhere—which might lead to a lack of enthusiasm or even regret as the decision doesn't fully resonate with their true energy—they wait to respond. Perhaps they hear a coworker rave about a beach trip, see an ad for a tropical getaway, or notice a friend asking for travel advice. Suddenly, they light up with excitement—that's their response! They know this is the right time and direction to start planning, and they'll feel energized by the process. By waiting to respond rather than

Response Indicators for Generators

"YES" RESPONSE	"NO" RESPONSE
Expansive feeling in your body	*Restrictiveness in your body*
Burst of energy	*A feeling of heaviness or burden*
A natural pull toward something	*Hesitation to move forward*
A desire to say, "oooh yeah!"	*A desire to say "ugh" or "eh"*
An immediate yes without thinking about it	*An immediate "no" without thinking about it*
Inspired, in awe feeling	*Feeling unsure, confused, or dreadful*
Making "uh-huh" noises	*Making "uh-uh" noises*
Your gears (gut) start churning in excitement	*Saying "kind of," "maybe," or "I don't know"*
Gut (area below your belly button) feels light	*Gut (area below your belly button) feels achy, heavy, and generally off*

initiating based on a whim, Generators can ensure that their actions are filled with energy and alignment.

Waiting to respond doesn't mean doing nothing. While they wait, Generators should do things they love—whether it's a hobby, a workout, or spending time with people who make them happy. When Generators are lit up and doing what they enjoy, they naturally attract even more of the right opportunities. It's like being in a flow state where life works with them, not against them.

MANIFESTATION TIP FOR GENERATOR'S STRATEGY:

Stop chasing—let life come to you. Pay attention to the small sparks of excitement when something external catches your attention. When you follow what feels good in your body, you'll align yourself with the energy of abundance and more satisfying experiences will flow in.

THE GENERATOR AURA: OPEN AND ENVELOPING

The Generator aura is known to be open and enveloping. It wraps around people like a warm embrace, creating a sense of comfort and inclusion. This magnetic quality draws others in, making them feel energized and eager to engage. To others, being near a Generator can feel inviting and vibrant, often making them the center of attention without even trying.

LESSONS AND DECONDITIONING TIPS FOR GENERATORS

Generators are designed to have lots of stamina and a deep well of energy to create and sustain. However, you often struggle with the misconception that you must always be active and productive regardless of what the work is. This can lead to committing to tasks that don't fulfill you and leave you feeling drained and frustrated as a result. The lesson is to do the things that genuinely excite you and say no to what doesn't. There is no virtue in being busy just for the sake of activity. You're the life force—that means you are meant to supplement and energize, not just to keep going without purpose!

Finding true satisfaction is another critical lesson for Generators. The endless energy Generators seemingly have is only evident when you do things you enjoy doing. It doesn't exist when you're forced into doing things you don't actually like doing. And because of this, you have the complete opposite effect on others if you're unsatisfied. A frustrated, dissatisfied Generator brings down the energy of everything around you, so it's crucial for you to be in a state of joy—we all feel it!

As a Generator, you also must learn the importance of listening to your Gut Feelings over the noise of expectations. You are often conditioned by people who assume the Generator can do it all because of this seemingly limitless fuel to go, go, go—but that Energizer Bunny only happens when you love what you do.

GENERATORS AT WORK

Generators excel in their careers when their work truly lights them up and feels satisfying. They need to feel energized and excited about their tasks rather than drained. Their best work happens when their day is shaped by what feels exciting to them, rather than just doing what is expected. By focusing on tasks that they enjoy, Generators not only benefit personally but they also positively influence the work culture around them. They should find ways to delegate tasks that feel draining to them to preserve their vital life force energy. Importantly, Generators should drop the idea that they must engage in activities that deplete them.

GENERATORS IN RELATIONSHIPS

In relationships, Generators bring lots of excitement and energy. They do best with partners who support them in following what makes them happy and helping them stay true to their joy. Generators do well with options, and a tip for anyone in a relationship with a Generator is to always offer them a choice. For example, if planning dinner, instead of asking a Generator "What do you want to eat?" give them a couple options, such as "Hey, which would you like, pizza or tacos tonight?" Generators are response-based beings, meaning they want something to simply respond to rather than come up with it out of thin air. The key is to know gut responses aren't always logical, so even if your fridge is full of things for taco ingredients but pizza is lighting them up—go with the pizza! This kind of support makes the relationship happier for both.

MANIFESTATION TIP FOR GENERATORS

Infuse your days by doing things that you love to do! I know it sounds simple, but in reality, I know it often is not. But believe me, this will unlock the juicy, warm energy inside you. Trust your gut feelings and let them guide your choices. When you follow what really lights you up, you'll be happier and inspire others too.

Manifesting Generators

The Multi-Passionate Powerhouses

ROLE OF MANIFESTING GENERATORS

Manifesting Generators are the dynamic powerhouses. They get the divine ideas that Manifestors get but also have the sustaining energy of Generators. They are designed to be multi-passionate and efficient at lots

ROLE
The Efficient Builder

ENERGETIC GIFT
Rapid innovation and efficient multitasking

STRATEGY
Wait to respond and inform

ALIGNMENT THEMES
Satisfaction (and peace) and frustration (and anger)

POPULATION
~32 percent

ALIGNMENT TIP
Let go of the idea that you have to do one thing

AURA
Enveloping and big

BIGGEST LESSON
Give yourself permission to pivot

FAMOUS MANIFESTING GENERATORS
Rihanna, Martin Luther King Jr., Lizzo, Harry Styles, Alix Earle

of different things. Manifesting Generators move quickly and can bring ideas to life faster than the other Energy Types. Their role is to find shortcuts and make processes more efficient through their hybrid energy.

THE GIFT MANIFESTING GENERATORS BRING TO THE WORLD

Manifesting Generators bring a unique gift of speed and adaptability to the world. They can pivot and change directions quickly, which makes them capable of responding to life's challenges with unmatched agility. Their energy is contagious and inspires others to keep up and adapt in fast-moving environments. When they are aligned with what truly excites them, they show us how amazing it can be to do multiple things at once.

MANIFESTING GENERATOR STRATEGY: WAIT TO RESPOND AND INFORM

The way a Manifesting Generator works with their energy combines the best of Generators and Manifestors. Their Strategy starts with "Wait to Respond," similar to Generators, meaning they allow life's possibilities to come to them rather than forcing actions or decisions. Like Generators, Manifesting Generators attract life and must wait for the right external triggers—be it a conversation, an event, or a question—to ignite their gut response.

Once a Manifesting Generator feels a strong gut response indicating "yes," their next step involves a key suggestion: to inform. This isn't a strict rule but a helpful guideline to reduce even more friction and create more spaciousness in their energy field. By sharing their plans or intentions with those affected, Manifesting Generators can pave the way for smoother interactions or pivots.

Let's say a Manifesting Generator is feeling unfulfilled at work and wants to start a side business. Instead of forcing an idea or randomly picking something, they wait to respond. Maybe they overhear a friend talking about a growing trend, stumble upon a YouTube video about passive income, or get asked by multiple people for advice on a specific topic. Suddenly, their gut lights up with excitement—that's their cue!

Now, as a Manifesting Generator, they'll likely want to dive in right away. But before rushing forward, they take an extra step to inform the people who might be impacted—maybe they tell their partner they'll be spending extra time working on this project, or they mention to their boss that they're taking on a creative hobby outside of work. This simple act of informing can help prevent pushback or confusion later.

Once they've responded and, if necessary, informed, they move fast. Unlike pure Generators, Manifesting Generators tend to skip steps, pivot quickly, and refine as they go—so they don't need to plan everything perfectly before starting. They might try a few different offers, realize one isn't quite right, and adjust on the fly. Their energy thrives when they follow their excitement rather than sticking rigidly to one path.

By using their Strategy—waiting to respond, informing when needed, and then taking fast, aligned action—Manifesting Generators ensure they're using their energy on what truly excites them while keeping their path as smooth as possible.

MANIFESTATION TIP FOR MANIFESTING GENERATOR'S STRATEGY

Embrace your dynamic flow—engage with what naturally draws you in. Notice when you're genuinely excited or intrigued by opportunities that come your way. By responding to these sparks with enthusiasm and then informing relevant people about your actions, you create a smooth path forward. This approach not only aligns you with your authentic energy, but also sets the stage for more fulfilling and abundant experiences to enter your life.

THE MANIFESTING GENERATOR AURA: BIG AND ENVELOPING

The Manifesting Generator aura is big and enveloping. It pulls people and opportunities into their energetic field. It combines the openness and magnetism of a Generator's aura with the boldness and intensity of a Manifestor. To others, this aura feels dynamic and expansive, often radiating a sense of excitement and possibility. People are naturally drawn to Manifesting Generators because their energy feels like a powerful current—warm, expansive, and full of momentum.

LESSONS AND DECONDITIONING TIPS FOR MANIFESTING GENERATORS

Manifesting Generators are designed to be multi-passionate and dynamic, but you often struggle with society's notion of staying committed to one singular path or finishing everything you start. One of your key lessons is to embrace your ability to pivot and refine. You thrive when you allow yourself to shift gears if something no longer feels exciting or aligned. Letting go of the need to "stick with it" helps you stay connected to your joy and maintain your energy.

Another important lesson is to stop forcing things and let your gut lead the way. Manifesting Generators often feel pressure to do it all or meet others' expectations, but your life force energy only flows when you're engaged in what lights you up. You must decondition from the idea that being consistent or finishing everything defines your value. Instead, you should trust your gut to guide you toward the right opportunities.

Manifesting Generators are naturally multi-passionate and thrive when exploring different interests. Trying to narrow your focus to fit conventional expectations can frustrate and drain you. You need to welcome your ability to juggle multiple passions as a unique gift, not a flaw.

Finally, learning to inform others is a crucial lesson. Like Manifestors, you benefit from letting people know your plans before jumping into action. Informing isn't asking for permission—it's about reducing resistance and ensuring smoother interactions. When you combine your ability to respond, pivot, and inform, you align with your true nature.

MANIFESTING GENERATORS AT WORK

Manifesting Generators thrive in jobs that offer variety, creativity, and the freedom to follow what excites them. They excel at juggling multiple tasks and moving quickly, but they must focus on what truly lights them up and delegate draining tasks. Their fast pace can be energizing, but they benefit from recognizing and valuing the contributions of others who may move more methodically. Letting go of the idea that they need to find "one thing" allows them to embrace their multi-passionate nature, while open communication ensures their dynamic energy aligns with team goals.

MANIFESTING GENERATORS IN RELATIONSHIPS

In relationships, Manifesting Generators bring spontaneity, excitement, and a sense of adventure. They thrive with partners who honor their variety of interests, encourage their passions, and embrace their fast-changing energy. Open communication is key, as they need the freedom to follow what lights them up while feeling supported. Their ideal partner appreciates their ability to keep things fresh and dynamic, offering a balance of autonomy and connection for a vibrant, fulfilling relationship.

MANIFESTATION TIP FOR MANIFESTING GENERATORS

Let yourself do it all. Your interests don't need to complement each other or make sense to others. Remember, your power lies in your dynamic energy and your capacity to adapt quickly. Trust your gut and allow yourself to pivot as needed without guilt. When you embrace your natural versatility and move toward what genuinely excites you, you not only achieve your goals more effectively but also inspire those around you to embrace flexibility in their own lives.

Projectors

The Guide

ROLE OF PROJECTORS

Projectors are the guides and advisors of the world. They are here to bring clarity and efficiency. They are naturally gifted at observing people and systems, seeing things others might miss, and offering fresh perspectives. Projectors excel at understanding how others can best use their strengths and at creating strategies to improve processes. Their role is to show us a better way.

Their energy allows them to connect with those who recognize their unique gifts deeply.

ROLE
The Advisor

ENERGETIC GIFT
To see and understand the big picture

STRATEGY
Wait for an invitation or recognition

ALIGNMENT THEMES
Success and bitterness

POPULATION
~22 percent

ALIGNMENT TIP
Prioritize rest and let the right people come to you

AURA
Focused and absorbing

BIGGEST LESSON
Focus on mastering your system or craft

FAMOUS PROJECTORS
Taylor Swift, Princess Diana, Gandhi, RuPaul, Marilyn Monroe

THE GIFT PROJECTORS BRING TO THE WORLD

Projectors have the incredible ability to guide others toward their fullest potential. Their intuitive nature and deep sensitivity make them exceptional at understanding and improving people and systems. They thrive when they are recognized and invited to share their insights, which can be transformative for individuals and teams. Projectors show the world how to work smarter, not harder, by leading with wisdom rather than force.

PROJECTOR STRATEGY: WAIT FOR AN INVITATION OR RECOGNITION

For Projectors, their Strategy is "Waiting for the Invitation or Recognition," which means they excel when others see their unique skills and invite them to share their guidance. Unlike Generators, Projectors are not here to respond to external triggers or power through tasks. Instead, their brilliance is revealed when people recognize their smart ideas and ask for their opinions, whether it's about friends, work, or big choices.

An invitation doesn't have to be formal—it might look like a boss or coworker asking for a Projector's help. This is the Projector's chance to share their thoughts. Because they were asked, their ideas will be welcomed and taken seriously. By waiting for this moment, Projectors use their energy wisely. They become valuable team members without feeling worn out.

In the meantime, Projectors do well when they spend time getting better at what they know, watching the world around them, and improving their ability to understand things. They don't need to do more just to show they are valuable—instead, they are at their best when they save their energy for times when they are fully seen and appreciated.

By sticking to their Strategy, Projectors can avoid feeling exhausted or bitter. They focus their energy on helping others in ways that feel right and

Invitations/Recognition for Projectors

ALIGNED	MISALIGNED
Getting compliments that genuinely reflect your contributions and insights	*Anything you feel you are forcing to happen*
Being asked for your opinion in discussions; acknowledging your expertise or perspective	*Feeling rejected by someone before sharing when your natural talents and insights are not recognized*
Engagement on social media when it reflects genuine interest	*Being solely driven by a need to be included or acknowledged*
Invites to social events where your presence is genuinely valued	*Imposing your opinions in group settings without recognition*
Praise for your achievements that recognizes your unique talents	*Sharing insights with those who don't value them*
A recruiter reaching out to you with opportunities that match your skills and aspirations	*Feeling bitter after initiating, then not receiving the recognition you hoped for*
People seeking your advice	

make a big difference. It's not about doing more; it's about being recognized and stepping into their role as trusted advisors when the time is right.

MANIFESTATION TIP FOR PROJECTOR'S STRATEGY

Focus on honing your skills and knowledge while you wait for the right people to recognize what you have to offer. You don't need to chase opportunities; the right ones will come when you're aligned with your natural wisdom. Trust that the universe will bring you invitations that feel like a perfect fit. Rest, reflect, and stay patient—your guidance is most powerful when it's truly valued.

THE PROJECTOR AURA: FOCUSED AND ABSORBING

The Projector aura is focused and absorbing, often described as penetrative because it can see straight through to the core of things. For example, have you ever been around someone who just sees right through you, like they just know things about you and get straight to the point of what you need to hear? This is likely a Projector. This is how their aura feels. I like to call it a focused aura because it has a way of staying concentrated on something long enough to deeply understand it or absorb all there is to know about it. This allows Projectors to understand others' needs, motivations, and energy. Their aura helps them see what others may miss and allows them to provide tailored guidance. However, it can feel intense if their insights aren't requested. When recognized, their aura is powerful and can change the lives of others.

LESSONS AND DECONDITIONING TIPS FOR PROJECTORS

Because Projectors absorb the energy of others, you often feel pressured to keep up with it. You feel conditioned by hustle culture, which results in intense burnout. Your lesson is to embrace rest. Your power lies in guiding others and offering quality over quantity. Letting go of the need to always "do more" actually allows you to thrive.

Another lesson: As a Projector, you should conserve your energy for the right invitations when it comes to offering your advice. You don't want to offer your brilliant guidance and not have it make a difference. This often happens when others don't fully see your inherent wisdom. If you offer your insights anyway, it can cause bitterness and take away from the already precious, scarce energy you have on reserve.

Learning to trust that the right people will see your brilliance helps you avoid burnout and resentment. Rest, reflection, and recovery are essential for Projectors to recharge their energy and show others the value of ease and alignment.

PROJECTORS AT WORK

Projectors excel in roles where their leadership and wisdom are truly recognized. They thrive in environments that allow them to guide, ask meaningful questions, and offer fresh perspectives. One-on-one settings are especially rewarding, as they can deeply connect and provide personalized advice. Projectors need regular breaks to recharge and perform best when their unique talents are acknowledged by managers and coworkers. Their strength lies in efficiency—they often complete high-quality work in just a few focused hours, rather than pushing through a full day of forced output. They flourish when given the freedom to cultivate their skills and interests instead of being confined to rigid schedules or output-focused roles.

PROJECTORS IN RELATIONSHIPS

In relationships, Projectors bring depth, insight, and a fresh perspective. They thrive with partners who recognize their unique qualities and invite them to share their thoughts.

Words of affirmation and being seen for their wisdom make them feel valued. Projectors also need partners who respect their need for rest and encourage them to work and live in ways that feel good for them, even if it looks different from societal norms. They feel most connected in one-on-one conversations and relationships where their observations and insights are appreciated.

MANIFESTATION TIPS FOR PROJECTORS

Stop trying to do it all. Your power lies in your ability to guide others and see clearly. Focus on nurturing your skills and passions, and trust that the right people will recognize your brilliance. Rest is essential for you—this isn't laziness but actually a key to your success. When you honor your energy, wait for the right invitations, and embrace your unique gifts, you unlock your full potential and create a life of ease, alignment, and recognition.

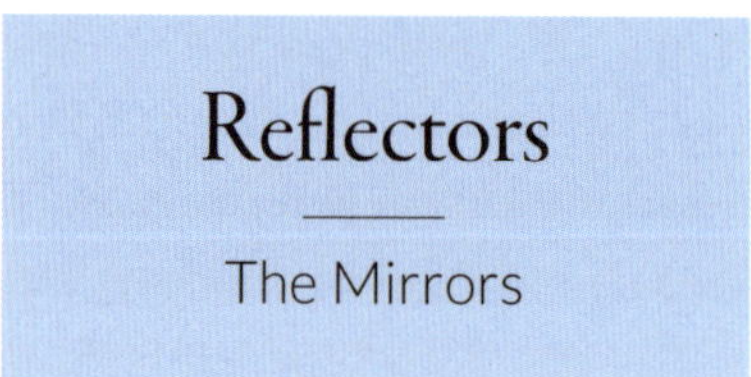

Reflectors

The Mirrors

ROLE OF REFLECTORS

Reflectors are the mirrors of the world. They offer a unique and unbiased perspective on how things are working—or not. As the rarest Energy Type, they are deeply intuitive, sensitive, and in tune with their environments, people, and even the cosmic weather. Reflectors act as facilitators, showing us the truth of a situation and guiding us toward improvement. Their role is to reflect the energy of their surroundings and help others

ROLE
The Evaluator

ENERGETIC GIFT
To reflect the health of their environment

STRATEGY
Wait to be included

ALIGNMENT THEMES
Surprise and disappointment

POPULATION
1–2 percent

ALIGNMENT TIP
Surround yourself with people and places that nourish your soul

AURA
Sampling and reflective

BIGGEST LESSON
Give yourself time—clarity comes through cycles, not speed

FAMOUS REFLECTORS
Sandra Bullock, Michael Jackson, Chelsea Handler, Amma, Rosalynn Carter

understand themselves and their systems more clearly. By embracing their fluid nature and letting go of rigid expectations, Reflectors can fully embody their purpose and bring clarity to the world.

THE GIFT REFLECTORS BRING TO THE WORLD

Reflectors bring the gift of nonjudgmental clarity and objectivity. They amplify and reflect the energy around them, offering unique insights to improve teams, communities, and systems. Their ability to sense what is working and what isn't makes them incredible facilitators and truth-tellers. Reflectors have a gentle presence and a knack for bringing people together in harmony, often serving as the heart of their communities. By expressing themselves in a multitude of ways, they show us the beauty of adaptability and how to live authentically.

REFLECTOR STRATEGY: WAIT TO BE INCLUDED

For Reflectors, their Strategy is "Waiting to Be Included" and being in the right place with the right people. Reflectors are like mirrors—they reflect the energy of the people and environments around them. To thrive, they need to surround themselves with spaces and communities that feel nourishing and enjoyable to them because these will naturally bring the opportunities they're meant to experience.

So what does "waiting to be included" actually mean? This means being in conducive environments where Reflectors feel seen, valued, and welcomed for who they truly are. For example, if a Reflector joins a new group of friends, they might notice how the energy feels before jumping into conversations. If they feel included and their unique perspective is appreciated, it's a sign they're in the right place. But if they feel drained or unacknowledged, it's a clue to step back and find a more supportive environment.

Reflectors don't need to force themselves into situations or chase opportunities. Instead, by simply being themselves in spaces that feel nourishing, the right people and invitations naturally come to them. Their energy amplifies what's around them, so when they're in the right spaces, they bring out the best in everyone; in turn, they get to experience the best opportunities.

The key for Reflectors is to trust how they feel in a space or around certain people. If it feels comfortable, they're likely in the right place. If it doesn't, it's okay to move on. Waiting to be included doesn't mean being passive; it's about trusting that the right connections will come when they're aligned with environments that nourish them.

Inclusion Indicators for Reflectors

INCLUDED	NOT INCLUDED
Feeling acknowledged and valued	*Feeling overlooked, invisible, or ignored*
Feeling comfortable and attuned to a space	*Feeling bypassed in conversations or decisions*
Being asked to contribute	*Not being asked to give input*
Feeling welcomed and appreciated	*Lack of invitations*
Feeling an emotional connection or bond	*Feeling uncomfortable or off in a space*
Being given the space to observe and reflect	*Emotional disconnection or detachment from a situation or group*
	Feeling rushed or pressured

MANIFESTATION TIP FOR REFLECTOR'S STRATEGY

Trust your sensitivity to guide you and don't rush decisions. Give yourself time to feel what's right and let the universe reveal the perfect timing for each step.

THE REFLECTOR AURA: SAMPLING AND REFLECTIVE

The Reflector aura is sampling and reflective. It constantly takes in and samples the energy around Reflectors, then mirrors the energy of the people and spaces around them. Unlike other Energy Types, their aura isn't intensely felt by others; instead, it feels everything around them. This allows Reflectors to taste the energy of their surroundings without becoming deeply attached. To others, their aura can feel calm, neutral, and deeply observant. It offers a unique sense of clarity and perspective. However, if Reflectors are in environments that don't feel good, they may reflect that disharmony, which is why being in the right space is so crucial for them.

LESSONS AND DECONDITIONING TIPS FOR REFLECTORS

Reflectors often feel pressure to conform or fit into societal norms, but your lesson is to embrace your fluid nature and trust the unique way you experience life. You are not meant to be consistent or predictable. Your gift lies in your ability to adapt and reflect, and your lesson is to celebrate your ever-changing perspective rather than resist it.

Another key lesson is learning to wait before making decisions. You may feel pressured to act quickly, but waiting allows you to feel grounded and certain in your choices. You must also prioritize being in environments and around people who make you feel like your best self, as your receptive nature makes you deeply influenced by your surroundings.

As a Reflector, when you learn to trust your process, you can let go of the need for certainty or definition and instead embrace the magic of your unique design.

REFLECTORS AT WORK

Reflectors thrive in workplaces where their insights are valued and they can work at their own pace. They excel in roles that allow them to observe and provide feedback, as their ability to reflect the health of a team or system is unparalleled. They are not designed for consistent output but instead contribute through their wisdom and perspective. Reflectors do best in environments where they feel appreciated and supported, with plenty of time to step back and recharge. Their adaptability makes them excellent at understanding group dynamics and pointing out what needs to change for better alignment.

REFLECTORS IN RELATIONSHIPS

In relationships, Reflectors bring a unique ability to mirror their partner's energy and offer deep understanding. They thrive with partners who appreciate their fluidity and create a supportive, harmonious environment. Reflectors need partners who value their reflections and insights without pressuring them to be consistent or defined. They do well in relationships where there is mutual respect for their need for time before making decisions. A loving, peaceful space allows Reflectors to flourish and feel truly seen.

MANIFESTATION TIP FOR REFLECTORS

Avoid trying to rush or force decisions. Your power lies in your ability to wait, observe, and reflect. Give yourself the time to experience the full cycle of energy before committing to anything big. Surround yourself with people and environments that feel good to you, as they play a major role in your clarity and happiness. Trust your process, embrace your unique way of being, and know that your wisdom brings transformation to those around you.

Reflection

Now that you've learned about your Energy Type, let's reflect on how you may experience it.

Do you feel like you're working with your Energy Type today?

Can you think of some scenarios when you felt most in alignment with your Energy Type?

Who in your life allows you to live closely to your Energy Type?

How could you let people in your life know how to best support you based on your Energy Type?

Does your current job support your energy?

Visualization

Visualize an entire day or simply just a scenario where you perfectly align with your Energy Type.

Write or draw it out, focusing on how you feel and the outcomes you experience.

"Intuition is not a one-size-fits-all experience. Each person's intuitive process is unique, and it can manifest in many different ways."

CHAPTER 3

FINDING *Your* INTUITION

In Human Design, your intuition is your *Authority*. We call it Authority because our intuition has the power to lead us to the right decisions. It's a deep, inner knowing—a feeling or sense that guides us even when we don't fully understand why. Many people struggle to connect with their intuition for different reasons. Sometimes we just get stuck in overthinking. Additionally, we've been conditioned to believe intuition should look or feel a certain way. But intuition is not a one-size-fits-all experience. Each person's intuitive process is unique, and it can manifest in many different ways.

The truth is, intuition doesn't always follow a single formula. It can be subtle, quiet, emotional, or even instinctual—and what works for one person might not resonate with another.

This is where Human Design comes in. It provides a framework that helps us understand how our intuition works. It explains that there are actually seven different kinds of intuitive Authorities, and each person has one that aligns with their natural energy. Your intuition may show up as a gut response, an emotional wave, a subtle instinct, or a deep willpower—let's find out!

Can you think of a time in your life where you made a decision that had zero logic but ended up being the right decision? For example, maybe you quit a job based on a deep inner feeling even though you had bills to pay and no concrete plans, but somehow, everything worked out. Or maybe you decided to move to a new city with no friends or job prospects. Or perhaps you were dating the "perfect" person and decided to end it based on a strong intuitive sense, and no one could understand why. Then, a few years later, you met the love of your life.

What I'm trying to say is that we've all had one of those moments, whether big or small, where we made a seemingly rash decision that people thought was ridiculous only for them to be proven wrong in the long term. Unlike impulsive decisions, which are often made hastily and without consideration, these decisions come from a deep sense of knowing and alignment with your true self. That's how our intuitive Authority works in Human Design. According to this system, there are actually seven different kinds of Authorities, and each person has just one primary Authority that they can rely on when making decisions.

Each Authority is linked to a specific Energy Center in our body; that area might also be influenced by external energies, depending on your individual chart. For example, some people experience their Authority through physical sensations in their body, such as a gut feeling. Others might notice behavioral cues, where certain words or inclinations feel more authentic than others. Additionally, some Authorities provide immediate guidance, while others require time and reflection to reveal what's right.

Here's a quick breakdown of the seven Authorities before we dive into each:

EMOTIONAL/SOLAR PLEXUS AUTHORITY
You need time to process decisions and gain clarity over time.

GUT FEELINGS/SACRAL AUTHORITY
Your gut gives you an immediate "yes" or "no."

INSTINCTUAL/SPLENIC AUTHORITY
Your intuition is fast and instinctive, often a quiet nudge.

WILLPOWER/HEART/EGO AUTHORITY
You're driven by what you truly want and desire.

VOICE IT/IDENTITY/SELF-PROJECTED AUTHORITY
Your intuition comes through speaking your truth.

ENVIRONMENTAL/MENTAL AUTHORITY
You find clarity by talking things out with the right people and in the right environments.

LUNAR CYCLES/OUTER/NO AUTHORITY
You need to give yourself time—around twenty-eight days—to ponder big decisions.

Reference your chart breakdown to find your Authority. What is your Authority? Fill it in below.

MY AUTHORITY IS ______________________________

Emotional/Solar Plexus Authority

Imagine you're riding a roller coaster of feelings every day. Sometimes you feel super happy and excited, like everything is awesome. Other times, you might feel down or sad, like nothing is going right. Emotional Authority is like having this roller coaster inside you, and it helps you make decisions based on how you feel after the ride smooths out.

HOW IT WORKS

With Emotional Authority, your feelings are like a superpower for making decisions. But here's the catch: You can't make a good decision when you're at the very top of the roller coaster (super excited) or at the very bottom (really down). You have to wait until the ride is calm, and you're back at base level, feeling neutral. This waiting time helps you see things clearly and decide whether something is really right for you.

Why wait? Well, if you make a decision when you're at the top of the emotional roller coaster, everything might seem like a great idea because you're so happy. But later, you might realize it wasn't such a good idea after all. The same goes for when you're at the bottom; everything might seem like a bad idea because you're feeling low.

Waiting helps you avoid these snap decisions. It's like giving yourself space to think about how you really feel over a little bit of time, not just in one high or low moment.

For example, imagine you, an Emotional Authority, are offered a new job. The initial excitement might push you toward an immediate "yes," but with this Authority, it's better to wait. Over the next few days, as you let your emotions settle, you observe how your feelings change. This wait helps you decide not just based on initial excitement or fear but from a place of emotional clarity.

WHAT TO DO WHILE YOU WAIT

1. Pay attention to how you're feeling. Are you super happy, really sad, or somewhere in between?

2. If you have to make a decision, don't rush it. Sleep on it if you can or just give it more time until you feel calm.

3. After some time has passed, think again about how you feel. If you still feel good about the decision—and not just because you're on an emotional high—it might be the right choice.

For example, say a friend invites you on a camping trip a couple weekends from now. Right away, you feel an immediate surge of excitement and want to say yes. But knowing your intuitive process requires time, you decide to wait a few days before committing. In that time, you sleep on it until you feel emotionally neutral. It turns out, it feels more like a no after all. Now you can let your friend know without guilt or regret.

TIPS FOR EMOTIONAL AUTHORITY:

- Sleep on big decisions.
- Journal or do a practice that gets you in touch with your emotions.
- Give yourself a day to two before deciding.
- The goal isn't 100 percent certainty, but 80 percent clarity.
- Tell people you need time to make a decision.
- If you feel like you know right away, still give yourself the space before committing (or not committing).
- Time is not meant for overthinking or weighing pros and cons.

- For small decisions (for example, what's for dinner) trust what comes up in the moment.
- If someone wants an urgent answer, remind them that your clarity on the matter will benefit them as well.

Gut Feelings/Sacral Authority

Imagine you have a magical light inside you that knows exactly what you want and don't want—that's your Sacral Authority, or in layman's terms, your Gut Feeling. Trusting your gut helps you make decisions in the moment. The really cool thing is that it's always working, helping you decide everything from choosing what's for lunch to deciding whether you want to move to a new city.

HOW IT WORKS

Your Sacral Authority is grounded in life force energy, which is a primal and visceral response system. It speaks through immediate gut feelings that don't require emotional processing or mental deliberation. The sacral response is binary and straightforward, primarily felt through physical sensations in your gut region (area below the belly) that guide you toward what generates life energy in you or depletes it. This Authority is characteristic of Generators and Manifesting Generators, who are designed to respond to life's questions with either a burst of energy (a "yes") or a lack of energy (a "no").

When something is a "yes": You might feel a surge of energy, enthusiasm, or a physical sensation of excitement. Your body will feel light, energized, and excited.

When something is a "no": Your body feels fatigued, heavy, resistant, energetically drained, or just plain blah, as if your body is conserving its energy by holding back.

For example, say you're on Netflix choosing between two movies to watch. One movie makes you feel super excited as soon as you see the image and think about watching it—that's your gut saying "yes!" The other movie kind of makes you instantly feel drained at even the thought of sitting through it—that's a "no" from your gut. Honor it!

TIPS FOR GUT FEELINGS AUTHORITY:

- If something is a no, it doesn't mean it's a no forever. The same goes for a yes.
- When you start overthinking a decision and get into your head versus your gut—you are about to decide from the wrong place.
- If you don't have a clear gut response, give yourself more things to respond to or have people ask you questions about the decision to help tease out a gut response. Remind people that binary questions (yes/no, this/that, A/B) are best for allowing you to tap into your gut.
- Remind people around you that trusting your gut benefits everyone.
- If you feel disconnected from your gut, start small (choose what to have for lunch).
- Try exercises or techniques that move you out of your mind and into your body and belly (yoga, breathwork, dancing).

Instinctual/Splenic Authority

Splenic Authority is like having an inner alarm that knows exactly what's safe and good for you in a snap. The alarm, however, isn't always so loud. Oftentimes it's like a quiet whisper inside you that quickly tells you something is safe or not before you even have time to think about it. This is why we call it instinctual.

HOW IT WORKS

Unlike Sacral Authority, which generates consistent and energetic yes-or-no responses based on how much energy you have for something, Splenic Authority operates through fleeting, intuitive insights that arise in the moment to guide immediate decisions regarding safety and well-being.

When something is signaling "yes": You might feel a sudden whisper, a gentle inner nudge, or maybe even an epiphany, tingle, or butterfly inside that makes you want to go for it. It's as if your body is quietly humming a happy tune.

When something is signaling "no": If something isn't right for you, you might feel a weird, uneasy feeling, kind of like when you think something might be a little scary or off. It might be a sudden sense of discomfort or even a bad taste in your mouth. You might not be able to put your finger on it, but you just know.

For example, say you're thinking about moving to a new apartment and you find one that has all the amenities you're looking for within your budget. However, upon touring the apartment you get this feeling that something isn't right. That's your instinct kicking in to let you know that regardless of all the great features, this just isn't your place. Trust it.

TIPS FOR INSTINCTUAL AUTHORITY:

- If you feel your instinctual urge to act, do it.
- Spend quiet time alone to hear your intuition.
- Go out in nature and observe how your intuition heightens.
- Try breathwork or meditation to get in touch with your body.
- Movement or any form of exercise can help you move out of your mind and into your body.
- Do not let fear drive your decisions. Fear yells, screams, and is loud in your mind. Instincts and intuition softly whisper. Know the difference.
- When you arrive somewhere or with someone new, notice the sensations within your body.
- Don't try to explain or understand your instincts—they aren't logical.

Willpower/Heart/Ego Authority

Think of Willpower Authority, formally called Ego Authority, as your heart's own decision maker. It's like having an internal coach that points you toward things that truly matter and bring you power. When your heart really wants something, this Authority will tell you that you need it. You have to have it. It helps you recognize which commitments and decisions are worth your time and energy based on what resonates strongly with your personal goals and values.

HOW IT WORKS

Unlike the Sacral, which is about immediate gut responses, Willpower involves the Heart Center and is tied to what you have the will or determination to do. It is more about making promises, commitments, and decisions based on what you can sustain and support through personal effort and willpower. This Authority assesses whether there's enough personal interest or drive to commit to something rather than just an instinctive pull.

A "yes" will feel like: an empowering determination or an inspired conviction that says, "I am fully committed to this!" It comes with a sense of responsibility and readiness to take action. You want to make a promise or commitment. You're driven and your heart feels in purpose.

A "no" will feel like: a lack of enthusiasm or drive, a disinterest in putting in the effort required. You may even procrastinate—that's your heart's way of showing reluctance or indifference toward making a commitment.

For example, you're choosing your major or career path in school. You've always been interested in psychology and becoming a therapist, but your parent is a lawyer and wants you to choose the same path. You know they make a lot of money and you are told how important this is. So you decide to pursue law to make your parent proud and start taking the required classes. However, early into the semester, you realize you have no motivation or drive to learn about law. You find yourself making up excuses, but ultimately, your heart isn't in it. You honor your Authority and decide to switch your major to psychology, where you feel a genuine drive and eagerness to learn.

TIPS FOR WILLPOWER AUTHORITY:

- If your heart isn't in it, let it go.
- Be intentional about your promises. Only commit when your heart is in it.
- Follow your heart.
- Remind others that it's not the best use of your time or energy to pursue something if your heart's not in it.
- It's important that your willpower and heart are respected and valued. You are not selfish for going after what you want.
- Drop the need to explain your decisions.
- Pay attention to what motivates you and why.

Voice It/Identity/Self-Projected Authority

Think of Voice It, formally called Self-Projected, Authority like having a microphone inside you. When you talk about what you're thinking or feeling, this microphone helps you figure out what you really want to do. It's kind of like when you start talking about what's on your mind and then realize how you truly feel about it.

HOW IT WORKS

When you talk about your decisions, your own voice helps you understand what you truly want. It's not about getting advice from others—rather, it's about hearing your own words bounce back at you. Here's what to listen for:

FEELING AUTHENTICALLY YOU: Notice how you feel when you talk about something. Does it genuinely feel like you?

YOUR WORDS: It's not just about talking; listening to your own words is also important. Sometimes, you'll hear yourself being really positive about one thing and not so much about another.

For example, imagine you're thinking about adopting a new pet but you're not quite sure it's the right decision. To help you decide, you choose to talk it out. You call a trusted friend, not for advice, but just to have someone listen while you sort through your thoughts. Your friend listens carefully, sometimes reflecting back what you've said or asking questions to help you further explore your feelings. You might also record a voice memo on your phone, talking through everything on your mind about getting a new pet. Later, you listen back to your voice memo and pay attention to how you sound when you talk about the pet. You notice that your tone is upbeat and cheerful, which signals that you're genuinely excited about the idea. Feeling assured by the positive energy in your voice, you decide to go ahead and become a pet parent.

TIPS FOR VOICE IT AUTHORITY:

- Processing things out loud is not crazy, it is necessary.
- Decide who in your life would be a good sounding board.
- When talking to others, be clear that you are not seeking advice, just support.
- Remind others you need to talk things through, and you are not overthinking.
- Listen for your intuition in your voice. Listen to what you say and how it feels to say it.
- Allow your words to flow out of you; there is no right or wrong way to speak.

- When you get the clarity, act on it (decide).
- Pay attention to when you get stuck in your head or veer toward overthinking.
- Invest in practices that allow you to express your voice (voice journaling, therapy, writing, art).

Environmental/Mental Authority

Environmental Authority means you make better decisions when you give yourself time and space to think things over in different surroundings. Similarly to Voice It, it's like trying on clothes to see which ones fit best, but the distinction is that you want to try out your choices in various environments and with different people to see which decision fits your life best.

HOW IT WORKS

This Authority really benefits from taking time and changing scenes or talking with different people. Each place and person can bring out different sides of you, helping you see your decisions from multiple angles. Here's how you can use it:

CHANGE YOUR ENVIRONMENT: Notice how you feel about a decision when you're in different places. A quiet park might make you feel different than a busy coffee shop.

TALK IT OUT: Discuss your options with various people who understand that you're not looking for advice, just a sounding board.

LISTEN TO YOURSELF: As you talk, listen to what you say and how you feel. Do you sound excited, hesitant, or indifferent?

Example: You're invited to be a part of a new project. You aren't sure about it and feel like you need to get out of the house to process, so you ask a friend to meet you at your favorite local park to walk and talk it through. You still aren't sure, so that evening you and another friend grab dinner at your local spot. It becomes evident through the different conversations and spaces that this decision is a no, as it wasn't feeling like you.

Like Voice It Authority, your voice is a powerful tool to tap into here as well.

TIPS FOR ENVIRONMENTAL AUTHORITY:

- Before making a decision, try out what that decision would look like with a few groups of people to see whether anything shows up for you.
- When talking to others, be clear that you are not seeking advice, just support.
- Surround yourself with the people who make you feel your best.
- Plant yourself in environments that make you feel most like yourself.
- When you get the clarity, act on it (decide).
- Pay attention to when you get inside your head.
- Remove yourself from places or people that don't feel good.
- Take time alone when necessary.
- Invest in practices that allow you to use your voice (voice journaling, therapy, writing, art).

Lunar Cycles/Outer/No Inner Authority

Lunar Authority, unique to Reflectors, is like having a special calendar for making big life decisions. This means giving yourself a full lunar cycle—about twenty-eight days—to really soak in your options before deciding. Don't rush this; use the moon's cycle as your guide.

HOW IT WORKS

Imagine you're deciding whether to move to a new city or to change your job. Instead of deciding right away, you take a whole month to consider the decision. During this time, you might visit the city or spend a day in the life of your potential job. You talk to friends and family about it, not for advice, but to hear your own thoughts out loud. You notice how your feelings change or stay the same throughout the lunar cycle.

This process allows you to see your decision from many angles and in different lights—just like how the moon looks a little different each night. By the end of the lunar cycle, you have a clearer picture of what feels right, without the pressure of rushing into a decision.

Another example: Say you're considering buying a new car and are unsure which model suits you best. Over the next month, you test drive different cars, research them, and discuss options with family and friends. Each interaction and test drive and the space to really process allows you to observe your consistent thoughts and feelings toward each option. This helps you make an aligned decision.

For more immediate decisions that can't wait a month, first make a temporary choice that you can change later if needed. This gives you some room to think it over more after you decide. You can also think back to similar choices you've made before or just check how you feel about it right away. Talking it out quickly with friends who listen well can help too. If someone is rushing you, ask for more time. Also, it's a good idea to have a simple plan based on what's most important to you to better make these fast decisions.

TIPS FOR LUNAR CYCLES AUTHORITY

- Before making a decision, try out what that decision would look like with a few groups of people to see whether anything shows up for you.
- Not every decision requires a full month, just the important ones.
- When you get the clarity, act on it (decide).
- Spend time in nature or in places that make you feel the best while waiting.
- When talking to others, be clear that you are not seeking advice, just support.
- Pay attention to what is happening in the cosmos (astrology, Human Design).
- Remove yourself from places or people with whom you don't feel good. Take time alone when necessary
- Invest in practices that allow you to express yourself (voice journaling, therapy, writing, art).

Reflection

Now that you know how your intuition works within your body, reflect on how this is alive within you today.

Think of a decision where you followed your Authority and one where you didn't. What were the outcomes of each?

What fears or beliefs might be preventing you from trusting your Authority?

How can you create a daily practice or habit that helps you tune in to your Authority more effectively?

How do you typically react when your Authority tries to guide you? Are you receptive, skeptical, or dismissive?

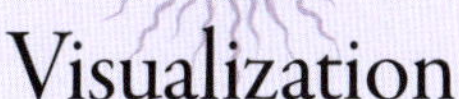

Visualization

Try this guided visualization to help you meet your Authority.

Find a quiet place where you won't be disturbed.

Close your eyes and take a few deep breaths to center yourself.

Imagine a space where you feel completely safe and relaxed. Visualize it in as much detail as possible.

In this space, see a figure approaching you. This figure represents your Authority.

Notice how it appears to you, whether as a person, object, etc.

Have a conversation with your Authority. Ask what it needs from you to make itself heard more clearly in your daily life.

Listen for any insights or messages it has for you.

Thank your Authority for its guidance, and then slowly bring yourself back to your current surroundings.

"Think of your Profile as your personality's unique flavor and how you express yourself."

CHAPTER 4

LOOKING *at Your* PERSONALITY

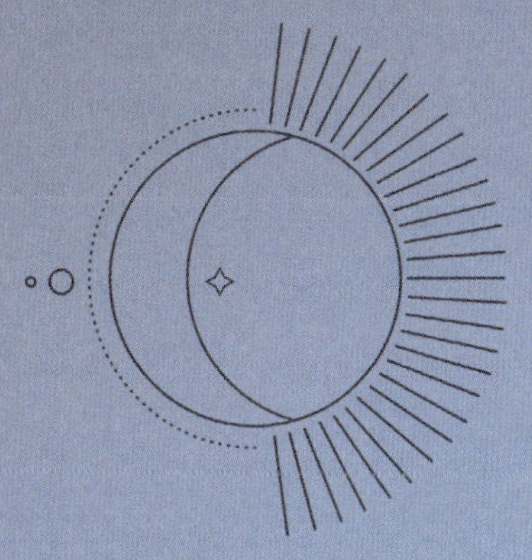

Think of your Profile as your personality's unique flavor and how you express yourself.

Your Profile is like the "costume" you wear or the role you play as you move through life. It's a key part of your chart that describes how you interact with the world, how others perceive you, and how you approach life's lessons and purpose.

Your Profile is made up of two numbers (e.g., 5/1, 3/5, 6/2); each one is known as a Line in Human Design. Each Line represents a unique theme or archetype, and together, these two lines combine to define your role in life.

- The first line represents the part of your personality you're most aware of—it's how you see yourself.
- The second number represents traits you're less aware of but that others clearly see in you—it's the part of you that works automatically.

The key to harnessing your Profile is to balance these different sides of yourself. I'll first introduce each of the six different Lines, and then I'll share some ways each of the twelve Profiles can achieve this balance.

Let's begin by uncovering what your Profile is.
Fill it in below.

MY PROFILE IS ______________________________

Line 1: The Investigator

researcher, Googler, knowledge seeker, thorough, foundation builder, detail-oriented

If Line 1 is part of your Profile, you're the ultimate researcher, the person who leaves no stone unturned when it comes to understanding a topic. You're the one everyone turns to when they need reliable, in-depth information because you've already done the homework—probably more than once. Your gift is building a solid foundation of knowledge that makes you feel secure and prepared to take on the world.

PERSONALITY SNAPSHOT

- Curious and detail-obsessed
- Loves to dive deep into research—Google is practically your best friend
- Finds comfort in knowing the "why" behind things

- Thorough, reliable, and meticulous—you don't just skim the surface; you dig in!
- Needs a strong foundation before making decisions or taking action

IN DAILY LIFE

Imagine this: You hear about a new health trend—maybe it's intermittent fasting, a superfood, or a funky herbal supplement. Instead of jumping on the bandwagon, you must know everything about it first. You spend hours Googling articles, reading scientific studies, watching YouTube reviews, and even diving into Reddit threads to ensure you've covered every angle. Only when you're armed with all the facts do you feel confident trying it out.

Or maybe you're planning a vacation. Instead of just picking a destination and winging it, you're the one creating a detailed itinerary and researching the best restaurants, hidden gems, and local customs to ensure an authentic experience.

Line 2: The Hermit

natural talent, introvert, independent, solitude lover, private

If Line 2 is part of your Profile, you're a natural talent, often gifted in ways you may not fully realize. You're the person who sings effortlessly and amazes everyone—except you were just singing in the shower, not thinking twice about it. You thrive when you balance time alone to recharge with connection to others who recognize and call out your gifts.

PERSONALITY SNAPSHOT

- Naturally talented without always knowing how or why
- Craves solitude to recharge and process
- Magnetic—others often see your gifts before you do
- Prefers to be "called out" into the world rather than being forced into it

IN DAILY LIFE

You might be deep in your own world—painting, writing, or just enjoying your quiet space—when someone knocks on the door (literally or figuratively) and says, "You're amazing at this—why aren't you sharing it with the world?" You shine when people recognize your talent and invite you to step out.

At work, you might prefer tasks you can tackle solo without interruptions, but when someone notices your skill, it can open doors for healthy collaboration. Balance is key—you need plenty of time to retreat and recharge before re-entering the spotlight.

Line 3: The Martyr

experimenter, resilient, trial-and-error learner, adaptable, risk taker, problem finder

If Line 3 is part of your Profile, you're life's experimenter. You learn through trial and error, discovering what works (and what doesn't) by diving in headfirst. In Human Design, the term "martyr" isn't used in the traditional sense of suffering or sacrifice. Instead, it refers to the experiential process that Line 3 individuals go through. While your path may be full of bumps and detours, your ability to adapt and grow through experience makes you wise, resilient, and relatable.

PERSONALITY SNAPSHOT

- Thrives on learning by doing
- Resilient and adaptable—failure doesn't scare you
- Relatable because of your life experiences
- Curious and always experimenting

IN DAILY LIFE

You might try a new workout routine, change careers, or test out five different ways to make the perfect coffee—all in one week! If something doesn't work, you move on, wiser for the experience. People admire your ability to dust yourself off and keep going, even when things don't go as planned.

At work, you're the one who figures out what doesn't work so others don't have to. You're a problem solver, and your wisdom comes from living, not just theorizing.

Line 4: The Opportunist

networker, community builder, relationship-focused, connector, influencer, stable

If Line 4 is part of your Profile, you're all about connection and community. Relationships are your foundation, and your success often comes through your network. You thrive when you're surrounded by the right people and focus on building genuine, meaningful relationships.

PERSONALITY SNAPSHOT

- Warm, approachable, and relationship-oriented
- Thrives on connection and collaboration
- Finds opportunities through networking
- Grounded and stable, bringing security to others

IN DAILY LIFE

You might get a new job because a friend recommended you or find your next adventure through someone in your social circle. Your relationships are your strength, and they naturally open doors for you.

In a work setting, you're the glue that holds teams together. You have a knack for fostering collaboration and harmony. You're not just about personal gain—you genuinely care about uplifting the people around you.

Line 5: The Heretic

problem solver, leader, strategist, visionary, rescuer, pragmatic, unorthodox thinker

If Line 5 is part of your Profile, you embody the role of a natural leader and problem solver. In Human Design, the term "heretic" does not carry the traditional meaning of someone who opposes established beliefs. Instead, it highlights your ability to challenge the status quo and introduce innovative ideas that bring about change. As a Line 5, you are seen as a disruptor, capable of seeing and suggesting new ways of doing things,

often ahead of your time. You are here to offer practical solutions to the world's challenges. However, with this role comes the reality that others may project their hopes and expectations onto you, viewing you as a savior or the one who can "fix" things. While this can create pressure, it is also a testament to your natural magnetism and the significant impact you can have as you manage these projections and navigate your path.

PERSONALITY SNAPSHOT

- A problem solver and fixer
- Magnetic and naturally influential
- Seen as a leader or someone others turn to for help
- Practical and focused on solutions

IN DAILY LIFE

Your team at work hits a roadblock, and everyone is stuck in frustration. Without hesitation, you step in, offer a clear, actionable plan, and get everyone back on track. You're the go-to person when people need guidance because you seem to have a knack for seeing solutions others don't.

Or maybe a friend is overwhelmed by a messy situation in their personal life. They come to you for advice, and you calmly lay out a practical way forward that gives them hope and clarity. People often see you as their rock—the one who can bring clarity to chaos.

At the same time, you might feel misunderstood when people project too much onto you. For example, you might provide an incredible solution, but someone criticizes you because it wasn't what they imagined.

This projection can feel heavy, but it's also a sign of your influence and natural leadership.

Line 6: The Role Model

---

wise, observer, mentor, integrity-driven, example setter, evolver

If Line 6 is part of your Profile, you have a unique life experience that the other Profile Lines do not. You're here to live life in three phases: experimenting (birth to thirty), reflecting (thirty to fifty), and guiding (fifty and beyond).

The first phase is from birth to about thirty years old, where you're in an experimentation phase and learning. During this phase, you live much like a Line 3 (The Martyr), experimenting and learning through trial and error. It can feel messy, full of ups and downs, and even challenging at times. This period is all about gathering life experience and figuring out what works and what doesn't.

The second phase is from around thirty to fifty years old. This is the observation and reflection phase, where you naturally begin to step back and review the first phase. It's like climbing onto the roof to get a higher perspective on everything you've experienced. This phase is about healing, observing, and integrating the lessons from phase one while focusing on authenticity and alignment.

The final phase is from age fifty and beyond. This is when you step fully into being the Role Model. You've gained wisdom from your experiences and become someone others naturally look to for guidance and inspiration. You're an embodiment of a wise sage.

Overall, the Line 6 is a natural teacher and guide, but your wisdom comes from living your own journey first. You're seen as a Role Model because you embody the lessons you've learned.

PERSONALITY SNAPSHOT

- Wise and grounded, especially as you age
- A natural teacher, guide, and mentor
- Seeks authenticity and alignment in everything
- Lives life in three distinct phases

IN DAILY LIFE

In the first phase, you're trying on different hats—exploring various careers, hobbies, and relationships. Maybe you take on a role in marketing, then pivot to graphic design, all while experimenting with a side gig as a yoga instructor. You learn through these experiences, even when things don't work out perfectly.

In your second phase, you find yourself pulling back and reassessing what truly matters. Maybe you shift to a career that aligns more with your values, simplify your social circle, or start a meditation practice. You begin to reflect on the lessons from your earlier years and focus on creating a life that feels deeply authentic.

By your third phase, you've become a Role Model without even trying. Perhaps younger friends come to you for mentorship, or you're the family member everyone turns to for advice. You inspire others by the way you live—your wisdom, authenticity, and calm presence naturally draw people in.

THE TWELVE PROFILES

Here are the twelve Profile combinations and some tips on how you can balance these two aspects of your personality.

1/3 Profile: The Researcher of Truth

Dedicate time to thorough research and investigation (1) while also allowing yourself to experiment and learn through trial and error (3). Recognize that deep understanding comes from both study and practical experience.

1/4 Profile: The Omniscient Teacher

Focus on in-depth research and understanding (1) while nurturing your network and community relationships (4). Use your connections to apply and share your knowledge.

2/4 Profile: The Introverted Extrovert

Honor your need for alone time and self-reflection (2) and also make time to engage with your community and close network (4). Balance between solitude and social connections is key.

2/5 Profile: The Reluctant Hero

Enjoy your solitude and personal space (2) while also being open to sharing your insights and solutions with the world (5). Recognize that your natural talents can benefit others.

3/5 Profile: The Experienced Hero

Embrace the learning that comes from making mistakes and experimenting (3) while also stepping into your role as a problem solver and guide for others (5). Your experiences make you a practical teacher.

3/6 Profile: The Philosophical Adventurer

Value the lessons learned from trial and error (3) and transition into sharing your wisdom and experiences with others as a role model (6). Understand that your growth journey inspires others.

4/1 Profile: The Genius Friend

Foster and maintain your network and community (4) while dedicating time to deep research and investigation (1). Use your connections to ground your knowledge and bring stability.

4/6 Profile: The Influencer

Engage with and support your community (4) while also embracing your capacity as a role model, sharing your experiences and insights (6). Lead by example through both your connections and your wisdom.

5/1 Profile: The Unique Savior

Embrace your natural inclination to provide solutions and guidance (5) while grounding yourself in thorough research and investigation (1). Be the practical problem solver with a solid foundation of knowledge.

5/2 Profile: The Self-Motivated Hero

Be available to offer solutions and guidance when needed (5) while also valuing your alone time for self-reflection and recharging (2). Balance helping others with honoring your need for solitude.

6/2 Profile: The Talented Role Model

Step into your role as a wise and experienced guide for others (6) while honoring your need for solitude and self-reflection (2). Your wisdom comes from both observation and alone time.

6/3 Profile: The Thrill-Seeking Sage

Embrace your capacity as a role model and guide (6) while continuing to learn from your own experiences and mistakes (3). Understand that your life's journey, including its ups and downs, is what makes you a powerful leader.

Reflection

Think back to your childhood. Are there any personality traits from this period that are highlighted in your Profile Lines? For example, I have a 1 (The Investigator) in my Profile, and I remember my mom saying I knew the most random statistics or facts. As a kid, I used to research whatever came into my head for no other reason than that's just who I am!

Is there one Profile Line you resonate with more strongly than the other?

How comfortable are you with people seeing you as the second Line in your Profile over the first? Can you embrace this perception?

We often lean in to our Profile when it comes to marketing ourselves in our career. In what ways could you use your Profile at work or in a job hunt? For example, if you have a 6 in your Profile, reflect on ways you can step into being a role model. Maybe it's by sharing your experiential wisdom through storytelling, offering case studies, or mentoring.

"Your dream life is possible.
But you can't get there
without having clarity on
what exactly it looks like."

CHAPTER 5

ENVISIONING *Your* DREAM LIFE

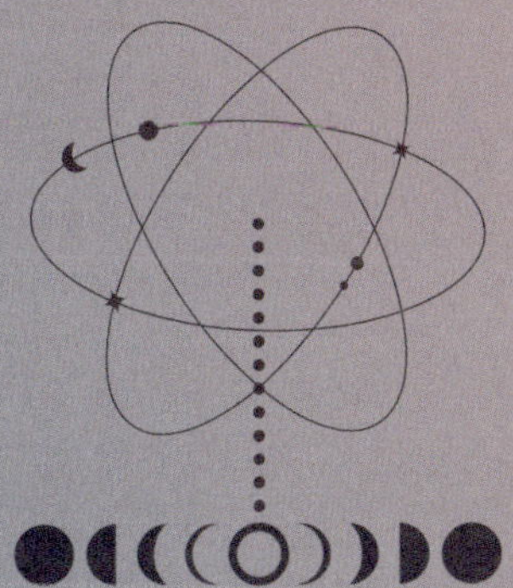

Now that we've covered The Big Three, let's take a moment to envision what's possible for you. Think of this chapter as a fun palate cleanser that will help you get more centered—and excited—about your dreams.

I know thinking about your dream life may feel overwhelming. Or perhaps it's fun for you—it can depend on the person. Either way, no two people will have the exact same depiction of their dream life, and everyone has a unique way of approaching this topic.

The most important thing to know is that your dream life is not farfetched or too big. In fact, I want you to go there. I want you to dream so big and boldly and fiercely. I want you to be a bit scared yet excited. I want you to dream.

Your dream life is possible. But you can't get there without having clarity on what exactly it looks like.

Now, as you read earlier, my dream life included working in wellness, living in California, writing a book, and helping people. Your dreams will most likely look very different from mine.

So how do you get clear on your dream life?

ASK YOURSELF:

What kind of life feels most fulfilling to me?

From the moment I wake up and go to bed—what do I dream of doing?

What makes me feel alive?

What am I truly longing for, even if it feels impossible right now?

Your answers are the blueprint for your dream life. And Human Design is the map that will guide you as you build it. Here are some tools to help you start figuring it out.

Visualization

This technique helps you see your dream life more clearly so you can get a glimpse of what your soul truly desires. Visualization taps into your imagination and allows you to create a mental picture of the life you want to live. The more vividly you can see it, the more your brain starts to recognize it as possible. It's a powerful way to connect with your dreams and begin aligning your actions with them.

Start by closing your eyes and walking through a day in your dream life. Imagine waking up in your dream place:

- Where are you?
- What does it look like? Is there sunlight streaming through the windows? Are you in the mountains, by the ocean, or in a city you love?
- What does it feel like? Think about the textures, the smells, and the overall vibe.
- Who's with you? Are you with a partner, family, friends, or spending time solo?
- What are you doing? Are you sipping coffee on a terrace, heading to a job you adore, or spending your day creating?

As you move through your day, visualize every detail: the clothes you're wearing, the sounds around you, the emotions you feel, and even the food you're eating. Let the experience be as immersive as possible.

Try doing this regularly, letting new details surface each time. You can pair this exercise with relaxing music or candles, or you can sit somewhere cozy to deepen the experience.

TO BUILD A PRACTICE

- Dedicate five to ten minutes daily to visualize your dream life.
- Write down the new details that stand out after each session.
- Create a "dream day" script and read it often to keep your vision alive.

Journaling

Journaling is one of the simplest yet most powerful ways to uncover what you really want. Writing allows you to tap into your subconscious and explore your deepest desires without judgment. It can help uncover patterns and bring new insights to the surface. Journaling is especially helpful if you feel overwhelmed or unsure about where to start—it creates space for your thoughts to flow and reveals what's been hiding just beneath the surface.

Use prompts to guide your exploration:

- If I could wave a magic wand, what would my life look like?
- What do I want to feel every day?
- What do I envy in others?
- What did I love doing as a child that I no longer do?

Write freely, without editing yourself or worrying about whether your dreams are "too big" or "unrealistic." The goal is to get everything out on paper so you can start connecting the dots.

ACTION ITEMS

- Choose one question from the prompts above or write about whatever feels most alive in your heart.
- Revisit your entries after a week or two and notice any recurring themes or surprises.

Dream List-Making

Sometimes clarity comes from seeing things in black and white. List-making is a straightforward way to map out your desires, identify what's important to you, and get a snapshot of where you want to go. It's perfect for those who feel stuck or need to organize their thoughts.

Start with two simple lists:

1. What I Don't Want: Write down everything that feels heavy, stressful, or uninspiring in your current life (e.g., commuting, working late hours, feeling disconnected).

2. What I Do Want: Flip your "don't want" list into the positive. For example, if you wrote "I don't want a long commute," your opposite might be "I want to work from home or live close to work."

You can also create lists based on categories like career, relationships, health, or hobbies, jotting down what your ideal version of each looks like. If you're struggling to identify these, use people in your life you admire as inspiration (these are called expanders.)

Vision Boarding

Vision boarding is a creative and visual way to connect with your dream life. It's all about gathering images, words, and symbols that represent what you want, then placing them together in a collage. Seeing your dream life in a physical or digital form makes it feel more tangible and keeps you inspired daily.

Start by collecting images that light you up:

- Use magazines to cut out pictures, quotes, and anything that resonates with your dream life.
- Create a digital board on Pinterest and fill it with photos of places, experiences, and aesthetics that match your vision. Make it your computer or phone background.
- Add pictures of yourself or memories that align with the life you want to create.

Once you've gathered your materials, arrange them in a way that feels inspiring and cohesive. You can use a physical board, a notebook, or an app like Canva to create your masterpiece.

UPLEVEL YOUR VISION BOARD

- Place it somewhere you'll see it every day (e.g., your office, vanity, or closet door).
- Make lists related to each photo and keep them somewhere close.

"In this chapter, we'll look at how you can use your Big Three to make aligned decisions—a key component of manifesting."

CHAPTER 6

MAKING ALIGNED DECISIONS

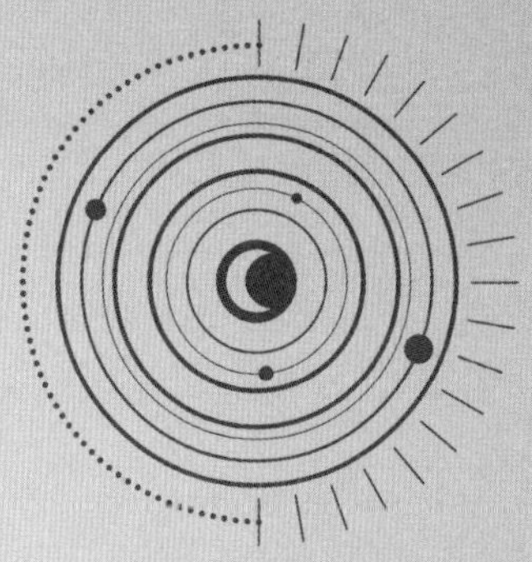

Now that we've spent some time thinking about your dream life, let's get into more of the detailed mechanics of Human Design so you can start to put Human Design into practice! In this chapter, we'll look at how you can use your Big Three to make aligned decisions—a key component of manifesting.

ALIGNMENT THEMES

Alignment Themes in Human Design are signals that show whether or not someone is living in alignment. Each Energy Type has a Signature Theme (the feeling you experience when you are in alignment) and a Not-Self Theme (the feeling you experience when you are out of alignment). These Themes serve as a guide to help you understand how well you're working with your energy or against it.

MANIFESTORS
experience *Peace* and *Anger*.

GENERATORS
experience *Satisfaction* and *Frustration*.

MANIFESTING GENERATORS
experience both *Satisfaction* and *Peace*,
and both *Frustration* and *Anger*.

PROJECTORS
experience *Success* and *Bitterness*.

REFLECTORS
experience *Surprise* and *Disappointment*.

Every decision you make and every situation you encounter can be understood through the formula

Strategy + Authority = Signature Theme

This formula is simple yet profound. When you follow your Strategy and Authority, you naturally move toward your Signature Theme—whether that's peace, satisfaction, success, or surprise, etc.—depending on your Energy Type. This is your body's way of telling you that you're on the right path and living in alignment.

Conversely, when you experience your Not-Self Theme—like anger, frustration, bitterness, or disappointment—it's a signal that something is off. This is an invitation to reflect and realign with your Strategy and Authority. Here is how each Energy Type makes decisions with their Strategy and Authority.

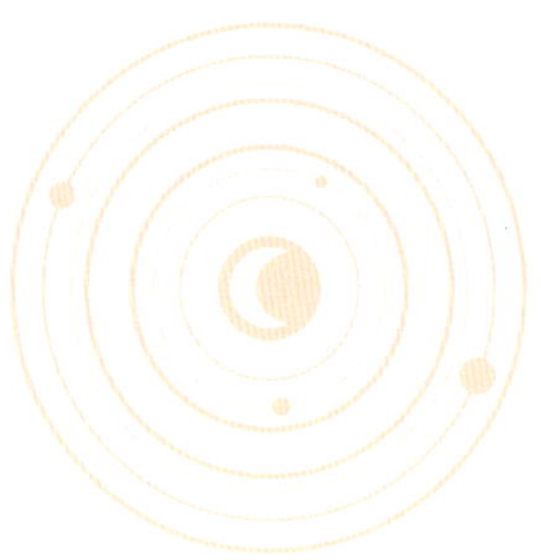

How a Manifestor Makes Aligned Decisions

Manifestors are first meant to sense an urge or impulse from the universe and then either . . .

- give the urge some time and space until you feel neutral (Emotional Authority)
- or open your awareness and pay attention to your instincts the moment the urge comes (Instinctual/Splenic Authority)
- or pay attention to what the urge is pulling your heart toward (Willpower/Ego Authority)

. . . then you will be ready to inform whoever will be impacted by this decision and you can finally move into action (initiate).

MANIFESTOR DECISION-MAKING FORMULA

STEP ONE: Get a spontaneous burst/urge/idea from the universe.

STEP TWO: Use your Authority (whether Emotional, Instinctual, or Willpower) to decide yes or no.

STEP THREE: Use Strategy of informing to communicate with those impacted.

STEP FOUR: Move into action and initiate your big idea.

How a Generator Makes Aligned Decisions

Generators are meant to wait for something to show up in their orbit (wait to respond) and then either . . .

- trust your gut in the moment (Gut Feelings/Sacral Authority)
- or trust your gut over time (Emotional Authority)

. . . to evaluate whether something is a yes or no for you.

GENERATOR DECISION-MAKING FORMULA

STEP ONE: Instead of chasing/forcing, use your Strategy to wait for something to show up in your world to respond to.

STEP TWO: Something does show up, as you're always magnetizing.

STEP THREE: When that happens, use you Authority to decide yes or no.

How a Manifesting Generator Makes Aligned Decisions

Manifesting Generators are meant to wait for something to show up in their orbit (wait to respond) and then either . . .

- trust your gut in the moment (Gut Feelings/Sacral Authority)
- or trust your gut over time (Emotional Authority)

. . . to evaluate whether something is a yes or no for you. Then inform those impacted.

MANIFESTING GENERATOR DECISION-MAKING FORMULA

STEP ONE: Instead of chasing/forcing, use your Strategy to wait for something to show up in the world to respond to.

STEP TWO: Something does show up, as you're always magnetizing.

STEP THREE: When that happens, use your Authority to decide yes or no.

STEP FOUR: Inform those impacted.

How a Projector Makes Aligned Decisions

Projectors are meant to master their craft and become an expert while waiting for an invitation or recognition (wait to be invited and recognized) and then either . . .

- sleep on it and give it some time to feel clear (Emotional Authority)
- or trust your instincts in the moment (Instinctual/Splenic Authority)
- or trust what your heart is pulling you toward (Willpower/Ego Authority)
- or verbally process it (Voice It/Self-Projected Authority)
- or process it verbally in different spaces (Environmental/Mental Authority)

. . . to assess whether an invitation is a yes or no for you.

If it is a situation that doesn't involve an invitation (for example, you have an idea about something), you can go straight to your Authority.

PROJECTOR DECISION-MAKING FORMULA

STEP ONE: Instead of forcing brilliance, use your Strategy to wait for an invitation.

STEP TWO: Use your Authority to decide if the invitation is correct or not.

How a Reflector Makes Aligned Decisions

Reflectors are meant to wait for an opportunity to emerge (wait to be included/invited/initiated) and then . . .

- take the time to consider whether it is right for you through cycles (wait a lunar cycle)
- for big decisions, if possible, give yourself a full twenty-eight days to decide whether something is right for you or not
- for small decisions, move at a pace that feels good for you and let others know you need a little bit of time and that it is for everyone's benefit.

REFLECTOR DECISION-MAKING FORMULA

STEP ONE: Instead of rushing, use your Strategy to wait to be included.

STEP TWO: Use your Authority to give it time and space to decide if correct or not.

DAILY ALIGNMENT PRACTICE

Human Design isn't just a concept—it's a lived experience. One of the most effective ways to integrate your Human Design Strategy and Authority into your life is through daily reflection, or what I like to call the Daily Alignment Journal. This is a concept I created (and it has since become quite popular in the Human Design world) when I began my journey with Human Design and I wanted a way to keep a record of my progress and energy.

The Daily Alignment Journal is a powerful tool that helps you track your progress, reflect on your experiences, and consistently apply the formula Strategy + Authority = Signature Theme.

Create a Daily Alignment Journal

Think of your alignment journal as a simple yet profound daily practice that keeps you connected to your true self.

1. SET DAILY INTENTIONS

Each morning, take a moment to write down a few intentions for the day, focusing on how you'll use your Strategy and Authority. For example:

- If you're a Manifestor, you might set an intention around being extra communicative with those around you, rather than keeping your plans to yourself.

- If you're a Generator, you might set an intention to stay present and surrender, rather than initiating action.
- If you're a Manifesting Generator, your intention may be permission to pivot when you notice yourself staying stuck on one thing for too long.
- If you're a Projector, you could focus on recognizing when you're invited to share your wisdom, rather than offering it unsolicited.
- If you're a Reflector, you might set an intention to observe and reflect on the energy around you throughout the day, noticing what pulls you in different directions.

This simple act of intention-setting helps you stay conscious of your energy and how you move through the day.

2. REFLECT ON YOUR SIGNATURE AND NOT-SELF THEMES

At the end of each day, reflect on how you felt throughout the day. Your Signature Theme is the feeling that signals you're in alignment, while your Not-Self Theme indicates that you've moved out of alignment. Take a moment to ask yourself:

- *Manifestors:* Did I feel peace or anger?
- *Generators:* Did I feel satisfaction or frustration?
- *Manifesting Generators:* Did I feel satisfaction (and peace) or frustration (and anger)?
- *Projectors:* Did I feel success or bitterness?
- *Reflectors:* Did I feel surprise or disappointment?

Describe specific moments when you felt aligned with your Signature Theme. Similarly, note when you experienced your Not-Self Theme and explore what led to that feeling.

3. TRACK DECISIONS YOU MADE USING YOUR STRATEGY AND AUTHORITY

Throughout the day, you make decisions both big and small. Use your journal to track key decisions you made and evaluate whether you followed your Strategy and Authority. For instance:

- If you're a Manifestor, ask yourself: Did I tune in to my Authority and inform others before initiating?
- If you're a Generator or Manifesting Generator, reflect on how you let your body's response lead the way with your decisions and how often you prioritized your satisfaction.
- If you're a Projector, record the times when you were invited to contribute or take on a role. Consider: Did I wait for an invitation or recognition before sharing my knowledge? How was my input received, and what was the result of waiting for the right timing?
- If you're a Reflector, reflect on whether you gave yourself enough time to consider big decisions before making them.

By tracking these decisions, you can start to see patterns in how well you're aligning with your natural energy and where you might be falling out of alignment.

4. EVALUATE YOUR ALIGNMENT

As you reflect on the day's events, ask yourself: How aligned did I feel today? Did I honor my Strategy and Authority? When you felt your Signature Theme—whether that was satisfaction, success, peace, or surprise—what decisions or actions led to that feeling?

Similarly, when you experienced your Not-Self Theme, what caused that misalignment? Recognizing these patterns allows you to fine-tune your decision-making process and make adjustments where needed.

5. BUILD AWARENESS AND ACCOUNTABILITY

Consistency is key. By journaling every day, you'll begin to build a stronger connection with your unique design and see how your decisions align with your energy blueprint. This practice will also create a sense of accountability, helping you stay committed to living in alignment.

As you continue to practice this daily alignment journaling, you'll start to notice patterns. You'll see how consistently using your Strategy and Authority leads to more experiences of your Signature Theme and fewer experiences of your Not-Self Theme. The more you tune in to your design, the more naturally you'll navigate life with ease, flow, and purpose. Your Daily Alignment Journal is here to guide you through that process, helping you create a life that is fully aligned with who you are at your core.

Reflection

Draw on each line where you feel the most aligned versus unaligned, based on your Signature and Not-Self Themes (Alignment Themes). For example, if you are a Manifestor, do you more often feel anger (misaligned) or peace (aligned)?

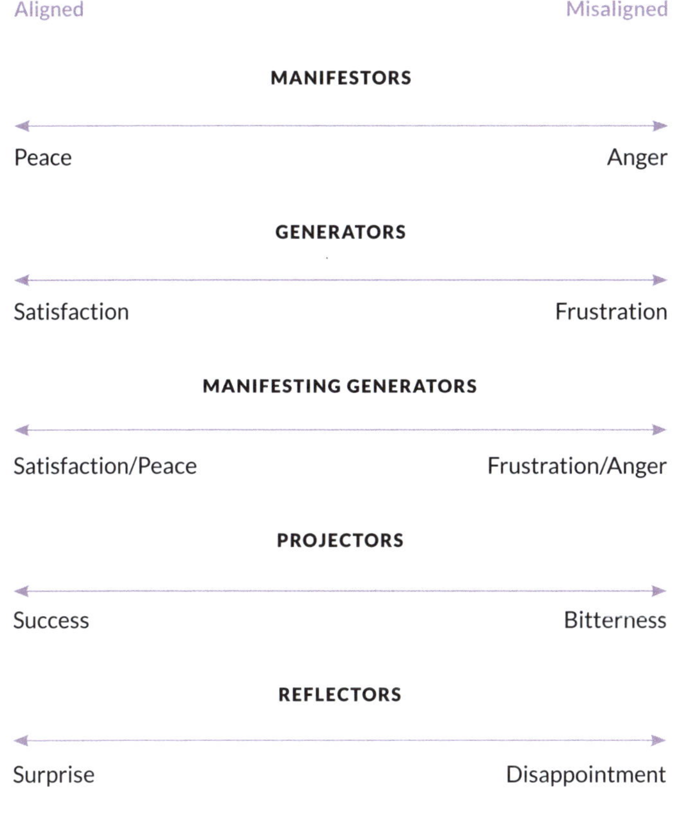

"This is where we're going to explore all the shapes within your chart and see how they are either connected or disconnected from each other. This part of your chart shows how your energy moves throughout your body."

CHAPTER 7

Your ENERGY LANDSCAPE

As we delve deeper into your chart, we're ready to learn more about your unique energy landscape. This is where we're going to explore all the shapes within your chart and see how they are either connected or disconnected from each other. This part of your chart shows how your energy moves throughout your body. We'll start by looking at your Centers.

CENTERS: YOUR ENERGY HUBS

Energy Centers are the nine different shapes within the BodyGraph. These are like hubs in a network, each governing a specific aspect of our being, such as emotions, willpower, voice, etc.

Each Center governs not only a particular function but also characteristics in your life. For example, the Identity Center isn't just about who you are—it influences themes of direction and self in your life and impacts how you see yourself and your path in the world.

By understanding whether a Center is Defined or Undefined, you can begin to understand where you draw your inner strength from and which areas might require more awareness, to avoid being swayed by external pressures.

Let's spend a moment figuring out which Centers you have Defined or not.

DEFINED CENTERS (COLORED IN)

When a Center is colored in, it's considered Defined or Activated. This means it operates in a consistent manner, always active within you.

UNDEFINED CENTERS (NOT COLORED IN)

When a Center is not colored in, it's considered Undefined or Not Activated. This means its influence is inconsistent and not always present in your life.

Grab your chart and color in the shapes that are colored within your BodyGraph. Note: If you're a Reflector, you won't have any Centers colored in!

UNDERSTANDING EACH OF THE CENTERS

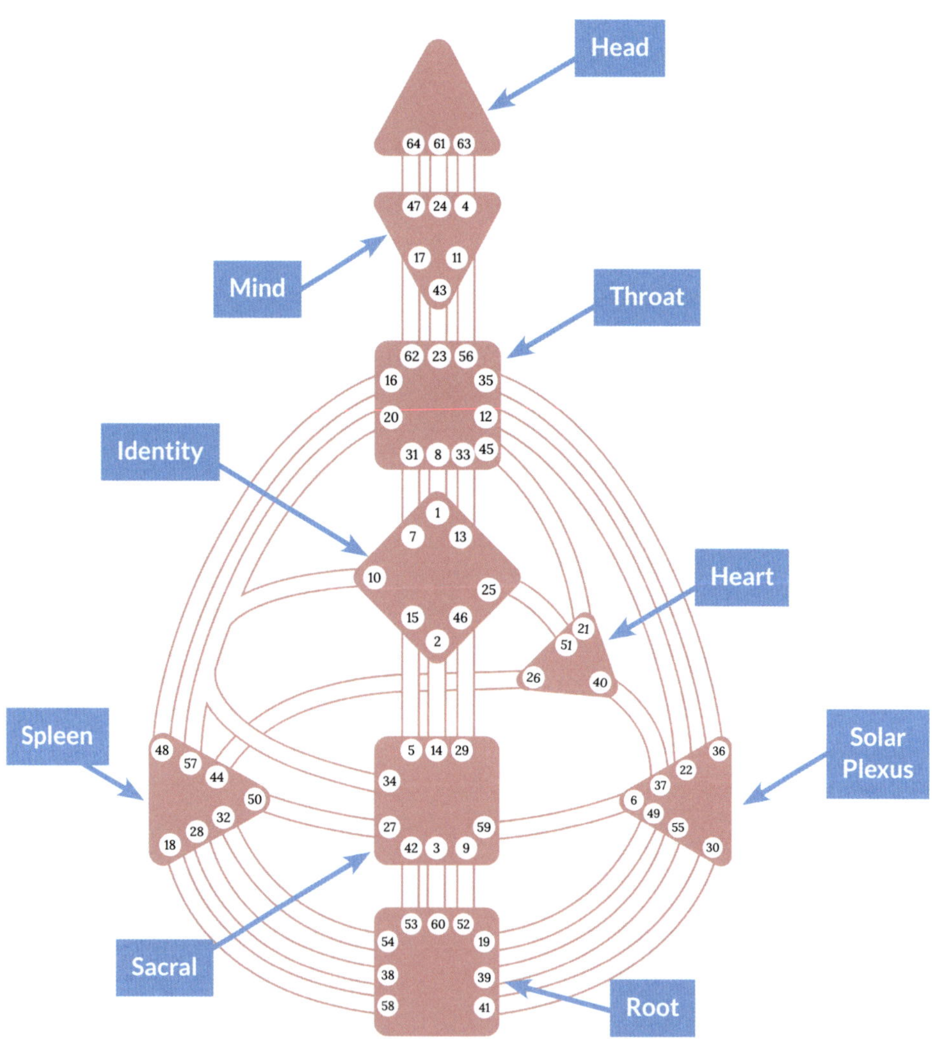

Head Center

How you get inspired and take in ideas

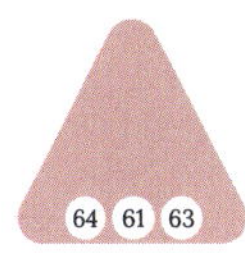

We begin all the way at the top of your BodyGraph with the Head Center, also known as the Crown Center. This Center is the source of your inspiration and the birthplace of your questions—it's where your ideas first start to form.

The Head Center is a pressure Center. This means it naturally pushes you to think, ponder questions, and seek out answers. It's less about finding immediate solutions and more about sparking your curiosity and desire to explore. It's often asking, "What interests me? What mysteries or questions am I drawn to explore?"

OVERALL CHARACTERISTICS OF THE HEAD CENTER

inspiration, the drive to question, thought processes, occasional confusion, generation of new ideas

IF YOU HAVE A DEFINED HEAD CENTER

You have a consistent way of processing inspiration and generating mental pressure. You may feel naturally inspired or have a strong desire to pursue answers to your own questions.

IF YOU HAVE AN UNDEFINED HEAD CENTER

You may take in and amplify the mental pressure of others, feeling like you need to answer questions that aren't even yours. This can create a sense of overwhelm or overthinking.

Mind Center

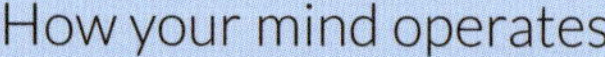

How your mind operates

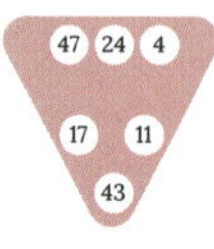

The Mind Center, formally called the Ajna Center, is the home of your thinking, processing, and conceptualizing. It's where you organize ideas, form opinions, and make sense of the world. This Center is all about analysis, logic, and mental awareness—it takes the inspiration and questions from the Head and works to turn them into structured thoughts and beliefs.

While the Mind can be a powerful tool for understanding, it's not meant to be the ultimate decision maker. Its job is to think, organize, and provide clarity—not to dictate action. It's often asking, "What do I think about this? How do I make sense of it?"

OVERALL CHARACTERISTICS OF THE MIND CENTER

conceptualization, beliefs, mental certainty, logic, processing, opinions

IF YOU HAVE A DEFINED MIND CENTER

You have a consistent way of thinking and processing information. Your opinions and mental frameworks are steady and reliable, and you're often seen as someone with clear ideas and a strong perspective. Others may look to you for your consistent mental clarity.

IF YOU HAVE AN UNDEFINED MIND CENTER

You're more open and flexible in how you think, which allows you to see multiple sides of a situation. However, you may absorb and amplify the thought and ideas of others.

Throat Center

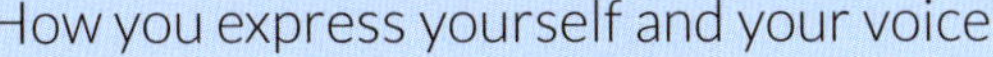

How you express yourself and your voice

The Throat Center is where your voice, communication, and manifestation live. It's the Center of expression—where ideas, emotions, and energy from other Centers are brought out into the world. This Center is how you make yourself seen and heard, whether through words, actions, or creative expression.

The Throat isn't just about talking; it also involves translating internal energy into an external impact. It's often asking you, "How do I express this? How can I share or create?"

OVERALL CHARACTERISTICS OF THE THROAT CENTER

communication, manifestation, expression, transformation, social interaction

IF YOU HAVE A DEFINED THROAT CENTER

You have a consistent way of expressing yourself and bringing attention to what matters to you. Others may naturally notice your voice or presence. You're here to share your truth and impact the world through clear communication.

IF YOU HAVE AN UNDEFINED THROAT CENTER

You're more flexible in how you communicate and express yourself. You may feel pressure to speak or act in ways that aren't authentic, especially if you're trying to get attention or prove yourself. Take your time, and trust that your voice is powerful when shared intentionally.

Identity Center

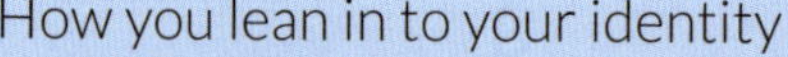
How you lean in to your identity

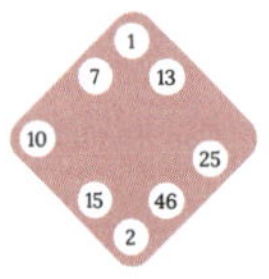

The Identity, sometimes referred to as the G-Center, is your sense of self, love, and direction in life. This Center radiates themes of identity, connection, and the journey of life. It's always pulling you toward your authentic expression.

The Identity Center asks, "Who am I? Where am I going? What does love mean to me?" It reflects your ability to feel love, offer love, and stay true to your path.

OVERALL CHARACTERISTICS OF THE IDENTITY CENTER

self-love, identity, direction, purpose, self-expression

IF YOU HAVE A DEFINED IDENTITY CENTER

You have a strong and consistent sense of self. You're naturally in tune with your path and your purpose, and your energy tends to attract the right people, places, and opportunities. You're here to shine authentically and you inspire others by being true to yourself.

IF YOU HAVE AN UNDEFINED IDENTITY CENTER

Your sense of self and direction can feel more fluid, as you're open to experiencing love and identity in many ways. You may adapt to the environments and people around you, which makes you highly empathetic. Surround yourself with people and places that feel good to you, as they deeply influence how you experience yourself.

Heart Center

How you get motivated and feel valued

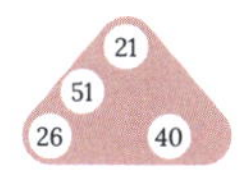

The Heart Center, often called the Ego or Will Center, is the powerhouse of motivation, willpower, and self-worth. This is where your drive to achieve and prove yourself lives. It's all about desires, commitment, and the energy to follow through on what matters most to you.

This Center often asks, "What do I want? Do I feel worthy? Am I ready to commit?" The Heart Center connects directly to material desires, goals, and the need to establish value—both in yourself and in what you create.

OVERALL CHARACTERISTICS OF THE HEART CENTER

willpower, self-worth, desires, motivation, commitments, value

IF YOU HAVE A DEFINED HEART CENTER

You have consistent access to willpower and drive. When you commit to something, you can follow through with determination, but it's crucial to commit only to things that align with your values. You know your worth and naturally inspire others to recognize theirs.

IF YOU HAVE AN UNDEFINED HEART CENTER

Your willpower and sense of value may feel less consistent. You might feel pressure to prove yourself or wonder if you're "enough." But your worth isn't tied to what you achieve—you're inherently valuable just as you are. Avoid overcommitting or trying to meet expectations that don't serve you.

Sacral Center

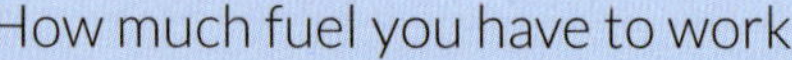

How much fuel you have to work

The Sacral Center is the life force Energy Center, governing work, creativity, and the ability to sustain effort. It's the core of vitality and response, generating the energy to do what you love and bring things to life. This Center responds to what lights you up, allowing you to say yes or no based on how your body feels.

The Sacral is always asking, "Do I have the energy for this? Does this excite or drain me?" It's designed to guide you toward fulfilling work and joyful experiences that keep your inner battery charged.

OVERALL CHARACTERISTICS OF THE SACRAL CENTER

life force, creativity, sexual drive, vitality, sustainable energy, response, joy

IF YOU HAVE A DEFINED SACRAL CENTER

You have consistent access to powerful, sustainable energy—when you're doing what excites you. Your body will always tell you what's right for you through a gut feeling (like a "yes" or "no"). The key is to follow that response and not overcommit to things that don't feel aligned.

IF YOU HAVE AN UNDEFINED SACRAL CENTER

You don't have consistent access to Sacral energy and may feel pressure to keep up with others who do. You're not designed to hustle constantly—you're here to work in cycles and take plenty of rest.

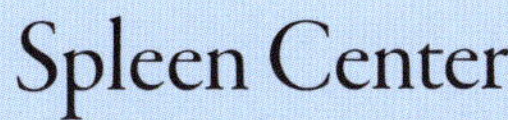

Spleen Center

How your instincts show up

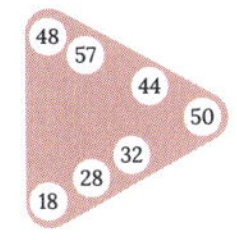

The Spleen Center is the home of instinct and survival. It governs your sense of safety, well-being, and moment-to-moment awareness of what feels good or dangerous. This Center is all about being present and in tune with your primal instincts.

The Spleen is always asking, "Does this feel safe? Is this healthy for me? What feels right in this moment?" It's designed to guide you toward what supports your well-being.

OVERALL CHARACTERISTICS OF THE SPLEEN CENTER

instinct, survival, well-being, safety, fear, health

IF YOU HAVE A DEFINED SPLEEN CENTER

You have consistent access to spontaneous hits of instinctual awareness. Your body gives you subtle cues about what's safe, healthy, or aligned. You may naturally know what's good for you without needing logical explanations. Trust those quiet, in-the-moment signals—they're there to guide you.

IF YOU HAVE AN UNDEFINED SPLEEN CENTER

You're more open to the fears, instincts, and health energies of others, which can make you highly sensitive and intuitive. However, you may hold on to things—people, habits, or environments—that don't serve you because they feel safe or familiar. Learning to trust yourself and let go of what's no longer good for you is key to thriving.

Solar Plexus Center

How you process emotions

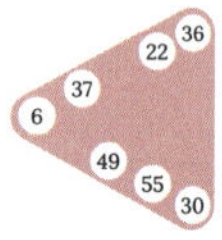

The Solar Plexus Center is the emotional hub of Human Design, governing feelings, moods, and emotional awareness. It's deeply tied to how you experience and process emotions over time. This Center is all about learning to honor the ebb and flow of your feelings.

The Solar Plexus is always asking, "How do I feel about this? What's my emotional truth?" It's designed to guide you toward clarity by allowing emotions to unfold naturally, rather than rushing decisions or suppressing feelings.

OVERALL CHARACTERISTICS OF THE SOLAR PLEXUS CENTER

deep emotions, empathy, sensitivity, emotional highs and lows, awareness

IF YOU HAVE A DEFINED SOLAR PLEXUS CENTER

You have a consistent emotional wave, meaning your emotions rise and fall in a natural rhythm. Clarity comes with time, so it's important to wait out your emotional wave before making major decisions. Your emotions are your guide, teaching you patience and deep self-awareness.

IF YOU HAVE AN UNDEFINED SOLAR PLEXUS CENTER

You're highly sensitive to the emotions of others and may amplify what they're feeling. This can make you deeply empathetic, but it's essential to practice emotional boundaries so you don't take on energy that isn't yours.

Root Center

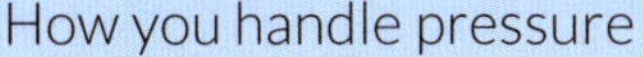

How you handle pressure

The Root is the Center of pressure, drive, and momentum. It's where stress and adrenaline originate, creating the energy to start things, get things done, and move forward. This Center governs your ability to handle stress and outside pressures.

The Root is always asking, "Am I ready to start? How do I handle this pressure?" It's designed to fuel action in a healthy way, helping you stay grounded while navigating life's demands.

OVERALL CHARACTERISTICS OF THE ROOT CENTER

drive, stress, adrenaline, momentum, pressure, grounding

IF YOU HAVE A DEFINED ROOT CENTER

You handle pressure in a consistent way and are naturally grounded under stress. You can work well with deadlines and know when to act or pause. However, it's important to avoid putting unnecessary pressure on yourself to constantly achieve—balance is key.

IF YOU HAVE AN UNDEFINED ROOT CENTER

You're more sensitive to external pressures and may feel a constant urge to get things done to relieve that stress. This can create a sense of urgency or overwhelm. Practice recognizing when the pressure isn't yours and give yourself permission to slow down. Not everything has to be rushed.

Centers Worksheet

Now that you have an overview of each of the nine Centers, let's explore how you can actively use this knowledge to enhance your life.

Think of your *Defined Centers* as areas where you impact people on a consistent basis. For example, if you have a Defined Solar Plexus Center, your emotions are felt by others. Or perhaps you have a Defined Sacral Center; in this case, people can feel your energy levels. Lean in to how your energy feels; this is where you can shine and show the world what you've got.

Think of your *Undefined Centers* as places to learn your greatest lessons. Since you attract and amplify the energy here from the world around you, it's important to reflect on whether this energy is serving you. For example, if you have an Undefined Solar Plexus, you may greatly feel the emotions of others and even have a tendency to carry these emotions, even when they're not yours. This can cause misalignment within yourself.

The way to move through this is by deconditioning and emptying out the energy in these areas. Emptying out involves managing their openness so you can gain wisdom from the experiences without feeling overwhelmed or losing your sense of self. Some practices in doing this are journaling, somatics, meditation, breathwork, movement, or even singing. Returning to your Strategy and Authority when making decisions will also naturally help you realign back to yourself.

If you feel particularly knowledgeable, experienced, or wise in one of your Undefined Centers, embrace this as your unique area of guidance and wisdom-sharing. For example, if you have an Undefined Throat, you might discover that you have a deep understanding of effective communication. Knowing this can empower you to help others express themselves more confidently and use their voices. When you lean in to your wisdom, you start to change the world around you and step into your highest self.

Reflection

How do your Defined Centers contribute to your inner strengths?

Do you find it easier to express the traits associated with your Defined Centers versus your Undefined Centers?

In which Undefined Center do you feel the most influence or conditioning from others?

Do you have any practices for emptying out your Undefined Centers?

Which Undefined Centers and their characteristics do you feel particularly wise in?

DEFINITION

Another key aspect of your energy landscape, Definition describes how the energy flows through your BodyGraph and determines whether your energy operates as one unified system or is split into separate areas that process information differently.

Think of it like a city's transportation system. Your Centers are the neighborhoods, and the lines between them are the roads connecting them. Depending on your Definition, your city might feel like one unified area or like separate districts that need bridges, buses, or other ways to connect.

This network impacts how you process information and energy, and whether you feel complete alone or when you connect with others. It also affects how you interact in relationships and environments.

Understanding your Definition helps you achieve your "flow state"—where you're most engaged and effective.

There are five Definitions: Single/Independent, Split/Collaborative, Triple Split/Synthesizing, Quadruple Split/Subjective, and None/Objective.

What is your Definition? Fill it in below.

MY DEFINITION IS ____________________

Single/Independent Definition

People with an Independent Definition are designed to rely on themselves. They often feel naturally whole and self-contained, as their energy flows seamlessly within them.

If we use an analogy of a city, think of Independent Definition as one unified, well-connected transportation system. Every neighborhood (or Energy Center) is directly linked, so there's no need for outside bridges or connections.

This consistent and self-sustaining energy flow means they don't typically look to others to help them process emotions or make decisions. They are self-reliant and have a strong sense of autonomy, which can make them feel more focused and directed compared to those with other Definitions.

Since they process information easily on their own, they are less dependent on outside input or collaboration. They tend to excel in situations where they can operate independently and follow their own flow without interference. However, just like a city needs regular maintenance to keep things running smoothly, it's important for people with an Independent Definition to carve out time and space to be alone, in their own energy, especially in environments that demand a lot of collaboration or social interaction.

KEY TRAITS: *self-reliant, consistent energy, autonomous, minimal need for collaboration, whole, focused*

TIPS TO GET INTO A FLOW STATE AS SINGLE DEFINITION:

- Carve out time for solo work.
- Minimize interruptions.
- Communicate your need for autonomy.
- Work alone/communicate that you're independent.

Split/Collaborative Definition

People with a Collaborative Definition have two separate energy flows in their chart that are not connected. Using the city analogy, imagine a city with two vibrant districts that function independently but lack a direct road between them. To bridge the gap and allow the districts to work as one, they rely on external connections—like bridges, buses, or shared spaces—to create flow and harmony.

This means Split Definition individuals often seek relationships or collaborations that help bring their energy together. While they can still process information and make decisions on their own, they thrive when others act as the "bridge" that connects their two districts. These connections can make them feel more whole and integrated.

Split Definition individuals are naturally designed to connect with others, and relationships often play a key role in their personal growth. When they're in partnerships or collaborations that help bridge their energetic split, they may feel more balanced and aligned. However, it's important for them to remain mindful of their own autonomy and avoid becoming overly reliant on others for validation or a sense of completion.

KEY TRAITS: *collaborative, relationship-oriented, seeks external perspective, dependent on connections for clarity, social, growth through relationships*

TIPS TO GET INTO A FLOW STATE AS SPLIT DEFINITION:

- Be around people to avoid isolation.
- Lean in to partnerships.
- Set up coworking dates.
- Work around others at an office or a coffee shop.
- Prioritize connection with others.

Triple Split/Synthesizing Definition

People with a Synthesizing Definition have three separate flows of energy within their chart. In the city analogy, this is like having three unique districts that are vibrant and self-sufficient, but not directly connected to one another. To bridge these districts, they rely on external routes—like traveling to new places or interacting with diverse people—to create flow and bring the city together as a whole.

Triple Split individuals thrive on freedom, variety, and movement. Their energy requires interaction with different environments and social dynamics to feel aligned and clear. Just as a bustling city benefits from open trade and activity between its districts, Triple Split individuals gain clarity by moving through diverse spaces and connecting with a range of people.

Staying in one place or engaging with the same group of people for too long can make Triple Split individuals feel confined or stagnant, even if they love the environment or people. Movement—whether it's a walk in the park, working from a coffee shop, or meeting new people—creates the bridges they need to access and synthesize all parts of their energy.

Their process isn't about rushing to conclusions but rather about allowing time to absorb and integrate the variety of energies they encounter. This dynamic way of operating brings them clarity and alignment.

KEY TRAITS: *flexible, adaptable, thrives in changing environments, needs multiple stimuli, independent but enjoys interaction, requires variety to feel whole*

TIPS TO GET INTO A FLOW STATE AS TRIPLE SPLIT DEFINITION:

- Move between different environments throughout the day.
- Avoid staying in the same place or with the same person all day.
- Take breaks to shift your energy when feeling stuck.

Quadruple Split/Subjective Definition

People with a Subjective Definition have four separate energy flows in their chart, making them highly self-contained and independent in how they process information. Using the city analogy, this is like having four distinct neighborhoods, each with its own identity and function, but no direct roads connecting them. These neighborhoods operate independently, and each one processes its own "business" without relying on the others.

This independence gives them a strong sense of who they are, and they aren't easily influenced by others or their environment. They process information at their own pace, in their own way, and on their own terms. Just like a well-established neighborhood has its own culture and dynamics, individuals with a Subjective Definition remain consistent and steady in how they navigate life.

To others, they may appear inflexible or closed off, but this isn't resistance—it's simply how they're designed. They aren't meant to easily adapt to others; instead, they are designed to honor their unique process, inviting others to adapt to them. Their predictability and consistency can be grounding for those around them.

Although naturally self-reliant, they thrive when engaging with a variety of people and environments. Just as distinct neighborhoods benefit from interaction with different parts of the city to add richness and variety, Quadruple Split individuals grow by exploring multiple close relationships and dynamic environments. These interactions help bring out different facets of their personality, allowing them to express all sides of themselves.

KEY TRAITS: *self-reliant, consistent, not easily influenced, requires multiple close relationships, processes at their own pace, unique, designed for others to adapt to them*

TIPS TO GET INTO A FLOW STATE AS SUBJECTIVE DEFINITION:

- Honor your need for space to process at your own pace.
- Seek diversity in relationships and interactions.
- Surround yourself with people who respect your process.
- Avoid forcing yourself to adapt to others.
- Invest in relationships that bring out your authentic self.

None/Objective Definition

People with an Objective Definition (only Reflectors have this) are designed to take in and reflect the world around them in a completely open and unbiased way. Using the city analogy, they're like an open landscape with no permanent roads or fixed neighborhoods. Instead of a structured system, their energy mirrors the activity, health, and flow of the environments they move through.

Objective Definition individuals act as mirrors, reflecting the energy and well-being of the people and spaces around them. They're here to observe, evaluate, and share unique insights without holding on to or internalizing what they take in. Their gift lies in their ability to see what others might overlook and provide a clear perspective that's rooted in their lived experiences.

They thrive when they allow energy to flow through them freely, rather than trying to hold on to or identify with it. Just as an open landscape changes and adapts to the seasons, Objective Definition individuals are designed to experience life from many different angles, gaining wisdom through variety and diversity. Being in motion—exploring different environments, communities, and relationships—is essential for them to feel balanced and aligned.

Staying in one place or with the same group of people for too long can feel stagnant, as their energy is fueled by new experiences and dynamic interactions. Their purpose is not to anchor themselves in one way of being but to embrace their fluid nature and share the clarity they gain with the world.

KEY TRAITS: *open, nonjudgmental, reflective, adaptable, thrives in changing environments, needs space to process, sees what others miss*

TIPS TO GET INTO A FLOW STATE AS OBJECTIVE DEFINITION:

- Move through different environments regularly.
- Take time alone to clear your energy.
- Avoid staying with the same people all day.
- Don't personify other people's emotions.
- Go often to your favorite, nourishing environments.

Reflection

By embracing your Definition, you can optimize how you engage with the world, ensuring that your energy flows as smoothly as possible. This can empower you to create environments and relationships that enhance your well-being and effectiveness. Let's reflect on ways you can use this in your everyday life.

At work, how do you generally feel throughout the day? Do you feel productive, disconnected, overstimulated, or isolated?

Create a list of changes you could make, if any, in how you work that would enhance your energy flow (a.k.a. getting into flow state) based on your Definition.

What don't other people understand about your Definition? How could you communicate to them how you best work and flow in life?

"When you know what your gifts are, you can stop second-guessing the traits that are second nature to you."

CHAPTER 8

UNDER-STANDING *Your* INHERENT GIFTS

Now that we've looked at your energy landscape and how you make aligned decisions, let's dive into your unique gifts. In Human Design these are called Gates and Channels. All of us have special gifts that come naturally to us and make us unique. Maybe you're a great listener, super persuasive, competitive, nurturing, community-oriented, or innovative—whatever your gifts, they make you you. When you know what your gifts are, you can stop second-guessing the traits that are second nature to you *Let's uncover how you can start embracing your gifts!*

GATES: ALL YOUR GIFTS

Gates are simply your gifts. I like to think of them as individual stars in the sky, each one shining brightly with its own unique light. Each Gate is a specific quality, strength, or talent that makes you special.

You can find your Gates in two places:

1. The Two Columns: Look at the columns on both sides of your BodyGraph. Each number listed represents a Gate you carry, influenced by a specific planetary energy. We're looking just at the number before the decimal point. Don't worry about the number after the decimal point for this book!

2. In Your BodyGraph: These are the numbers colored in on your BodyGraph chart, each with a line extending from it out to one of your Energy Centers.

Let's begin by filling out each of your Gates.

You may have noticed the different planetary symbols next to your Gates. This is because each of your 26 Gates has a cosmic influence from the celestial bodies and planets they were in when you were born. Since our Gates show us our gifts, you can use the planetary influence each one is in to understand even more about how these gifts show up in your life.

Each planet will have two Gates within it from the unconscious and conscious sides of your chart. On the next page is a breakdown of what each one means.

One last thing before we move through each Gate: Know that each of the Gates has a quality that can be expressed in different ways depending on your awareness and how aligned you are.

The *high expression* of a Gate is its most aligned, empowered, and evolved state. It represents how the energy of that Gate shines when you're in alignment with your design and using your gifts in a way that serves you and others. When you're in the high expression, you're embodying the gift of the Gate with clarity and confidence, often making a positive impact on others.

The *low expression* of a Gate occurs when its energy is influenced by fear, conditioning, or misalignment. Instead of being empowering, the energy may feel restrictive, chaotic, or misdirected. The low expression isn't "bad"—it's simply a signpost showing where you might need awareness or a shift in perspective to move toward alignment.

Let's move through each of the 64 Gates and what it means to be in the high or low expression of each. We have included a check circle beside each Gate for you to mark whether you have it or not.

Planetary Themes

SUN	☉	your core energy, personal power, and talent
EARTH	⊕	what grounds you and brings you stability
NORTH NODE	☊	your future direction, soul's purpose, and expression of wisdom from age forty onward
SOUTH NODE	☋	past-life energy and what you are here to further integrate from age zero to thirty-nine
MOON	☽	what drives you in life
MERCURY	☿	what you are here to communicate and share
VENUS	♀	Your moral values and what you love
MARS	♂	where you have the opportunity to mature and grow in this lifetime
JUPITER	♃	the gifts to lean in to in order to be well rewarded in this lifetime
SATURN	♄	where you learn to take responsibility and are shown the consequences of your own behavior (good or bad)
URANUS	⛢	where you deviate from the norm and do things a little differently
NEPTUNE	♆	your spiritual work and what brings you joy
PLUTO	♇	your underlying truth, shadow work, and inner transformation
CHIRON	⚷	your deepest wound; where you are meant to heal and help others heal through your own wisdom

Gate 1—Creativity ○

Innate Creativity, Self-Expression, Newness, Beauty, Independence, Natural Cycles

GIFT: Divine creativity

HIGH EXPRESSION: Embodying self-expression and creativity without an agenda, bringing fresh perspectives and newness. Authentic expression empowers others to do the same, creating a sense of beauty that is indescribable through one's essence.

LOW EXPRESSION: Feeling stagnant in creative pursuits and unsure of how to express oneself. Potential for depression due to a lack of self-expression and impatience with the creative process.

Gate 2—Vision ○

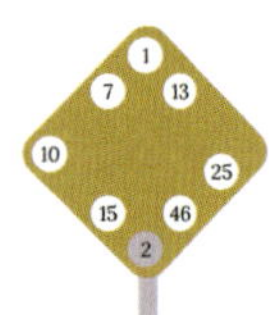

Being a Visionary, Receptivity, Adaptability, Higher Knowing, Abundance, Direction

GIFT: Possessing a deep inner sense of direction

HIGH EXPRESSION: Guided by a profound inner knowing of where to go and how to navigate life. Trusting in the flow of life and naturally aligning with one's path, attracting the right opportunities.

LOW EXPRESSION: Feeling lost or directionless, struggling to find one's path. Potential to depend too much on external guidance and lack confidence in navigating life's course.

Gate 3—Order ○

Innovation, Transformation, Newness, Initiation, Leaps of Faith, Making Order Out of Chaos

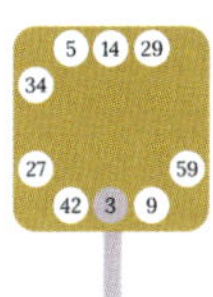

GIFT: A natural innovator, bringing order to chaos

HIGH EXPRESSION: Embracing change and creating order from disorder. Adaptable and pioneering new ways and processes, helping others find structure in the chaos.

LOW EXPRESSION: Resisting change and feeling overwhelmed by chaotic situations. Struggling to see the potential for new beginnings and becoming stuck in outdated patterns.

Gate 4—Understanding

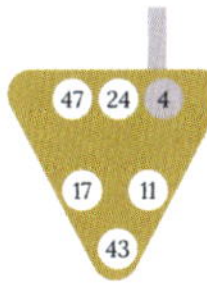

Understanding, Love of Logic, Mental Solutions, Possibility, Forgiveness

GIFT: Logical thinking and problem-solving

HIGH EXPRESSION: Providing answers and solutions with clarity and insight. Helping others see logical pathways forward and bringing understanding to complex problems.

LOW EXPRESSION: Becoming overly dependent on finding answers and feeling anxious without certainty. Getting stuck in mental loops and overthinking.

Gate 5—Rhythm

Fixed Rhythms, Rituals, Routines, Habits

GIFT: Attuned to the natural rhythms of life

HIGH EXPRESSION: Having stability in healthy routines.

LOW EXPRESSION: Resisting change and becoming too rigid in routines.

Gate 6—Discernment

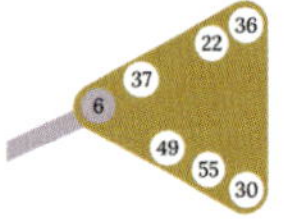

Being Discerning, Conflict, Inner Peace, Resolution

GIFT: Master of emotional clarity and healthy boundaries

HIGH EXPRESSION: Navigating emotional dynamics with grace and resolving conflicts adeptly. Creating deeper emotional bonds by understanding one's own emotions and those of others.

LOW EXPRESSION: Experiencing emotional confusion and conflict, avoiding confrontation or becoming overly defensive. Struggling with setting or respecting boundaries.

Gate 7—The Leader

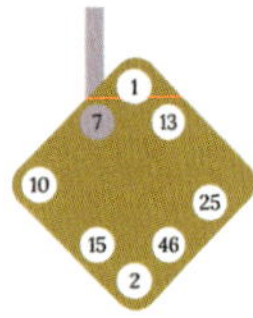

Natural Leader, Guidance, Empowerment

GIFT: A natural talent for leadership

HIGH EXPRESSION: Guiding others with integrity, vision, and collaboration. Excelling at leading teams or groups toward collective goals, embodying a servant-leader mindset.

LOW EXPRESSION: Becoming overly controlling or struggling with a need for recognition. Getting caught in power struggles, losing sight of collaborative leadership.

Gate 8—Contribution

Making a Contribution, Natural Tastemaker, Grabbing Attention, Authenticity

GIFT: Uniquely expressive, inspiring others to find their own voice

HIGH EXPRESSION: Standing out by expressing individuality and encouraging others to do the same. Influential in helping others see the value of being authentic and unique.

LOW EXPRESSION: Becoming attention-seeking or feeling unrecognized for uniqueness. Struggling with feeling out of place or that contributions are undervalued.

Gate 9—Focus

Determination, Focus, Concentration, Seeing

GIFT: Ability to focus on details and stay committed to tasks

HIGH EXPRESSION: Bringing clarity through focused attention and having the patience to work through details meticulously. Excelling at breaking down big projects into manageable steps.

LOW EXPRESSION: Becoming overly focused on minor details, missing the bigger picture. Feeling overwhelmed or stuck in trivial matters, leading to a lack of progress.

Gate 10—Self-Love

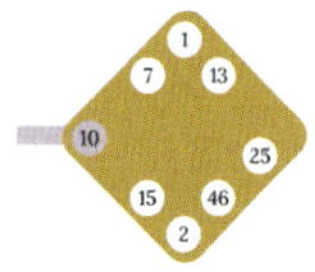

Self-Love, Empowerment, Being an Example

GIFT: Embodying a deep sense of self-love and authenticity

HIGH EXPRESSION: Modeling self-acceptance and encouraging others to be true to themselves. Behavior reflects inner alignment that inspires others to embrace their uniqueness.

LOW EXPRESSION: Struggling with self-judgment or feeling disconnected from the true self. Conforming to external expectations, leading to dissatisfaction and lack of authenticity.

Gate 11—Ideas ○

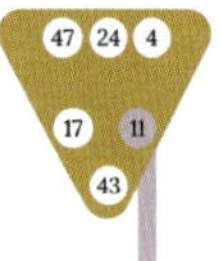

Ideation, Peace, Inner Contemplation, Imagination, Visualization

GIFT: Vivid ideas and visions

HIGH EXPRESSION: Generating new ideas and sharing them in ways that inspire others. Bringing creative and visionary thinking that offers fresh perspectives to groups and communities.

LOW EXPRESSION: Feeling overwhelmed by too many ideas without a clear way to manifest them. Struggling with indecision or feeling ungrounded in thinking.

Gate 12—Articulation ○

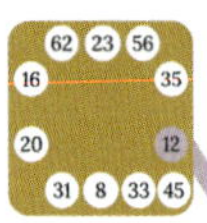

Caution, Restraint, Good Taste, Refined Expression Verbally and Artistically

GIFT: Talent for impactful communication

HIGH EXPRESSION: Communicating with depth and authenticity, knowing when to speak and when to remain silent. Powerfully influencing others with words.

LOW EXPRESSION: Fearing expressing oneself or feeling misunderstood. Being overly cautious in communication, leading to missed opportunities for meaningful dialogue.

Gate 13—Listening ○

Being a Listener, Empathetic, Forgiveness, Keeping Secrets

GIFT: Ability to deeply listen and retain stories

HIGH EXPRESSION: Holding space for others to share their stories and experiences, providing wisdom when the time is

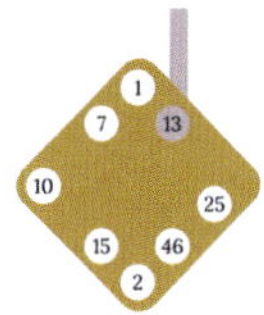

right. Trusted confidants with a knack for understanding human dynamics.

LOW EXPRESSION: Feeling burdened by others' stories or overwhelmed by what is heard. Struggling with knowing when and how to share what has been learned.

Gate 14—Prosperity

Power Skills, Generously Giving, Successful Interactions

GIFT: Naturally attuned to generating and managing resources

HIGH EXPRESSION: Attracting abundance and using it wisely. Skilled at recognizing potential in opportunities and maximizing them for growth.

LOW EXPRESSION: Feeling powerless or undervalued, struggling with a scarcity mindset. Misusing resources or failing to see opportunities in the environment.

Gate 15—Extremes

Extremes, Lack of Routine, Personal Rhythm, Radical Authenticity, Wild

GIFT: Comfortable embracing extremes and diversity

HIGH EXPRESSION: Flowing with the diversity of life, accepting all ranges of experiences. Bringing balance by navigating extremes with grace and understanding.

LOW EXPRESSION: Feeling disconnected or too different from others; becoming isolated or erratic. Struggling with being too extreme or too conforming, depending on circumstances.

Gate 16—Skills ○

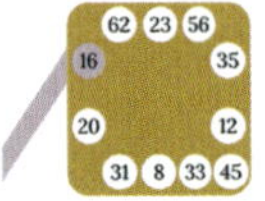

Skills, Enthusiasm, Talent, Mastery

GIFT: Natural talent for refining and mastering skills

HIGH EXPRESSION: Enthusiastic about learning and developing skills, sharing them with the world in creative ways. Inspiring others through dedication to mastery and continuous improvement.

LOW EXPRESSION: Feeling inadequate or fearing that skills are not good enough. Becoming scattered, trying to learn too many things at once without committing to mastery.

Gate 17—Solutions ○

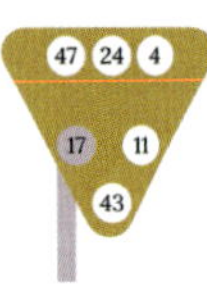

Opinions, Solutions, Logical, Doubtful, Skeptical, Pattern Seeker

GIFT: Insightful with a natural ability to form logical opinions

HIGH EXPRESSION: Providing valuable insights and perspectives that help improve understanding and decision-making within groups. Presenting opinions in a way that invites discussion and growth.

LOW EXPRESSION: Coming across as overly critical or rigid in thinking. Struggling with needing to be right or feeling dismissed when opinions are not accepted.

Gate 18—Correcting ○

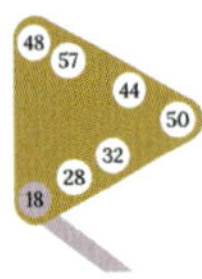

Critiquing, Correcting, Perfecting, Wholeness, Clear Seeing

GIFT: Ability to see what needs improvement

HIGH EXPRESSION: Skilled at identifying flaws and making constructive corrections. Bringing a sense of refinement and betterment to systems and relationships.

LOW EXPRESSION: Becoming overly critical of oneself or others, focusing too much on imperfections. Struggling with feeling responsible for fixing everything.

Gate 19—Sensitivity

Strong Principles, Morals, Sensitivity, Needs Attunement, Uplifting Community

GIFT: Highly sensitive to the needs of others and the environment

HIGH EXPRESSION: Intuitively knowing what is needed for emotional and physical well-being. Empathetic and supportive, fostering a sense of belonging and care.

LOW EXPRESSION: Feeling overly dependent on others for emotional support. Struggling with feeling overly sensitive or needy, leading to codependency.

Gate 20—Presence

Presence, Contemplation, Alchemy, This Moment

GIFT: Being fully present in the moment

HIGH EXPRESSION: Acting and speaking from a place of truth in the here and now. Possessing a powerful presence that influences others and brings immediate clarity and action.

LOW EXPRESSION: Struggling with impulsivity or lack of follow-through. Feeling disconnected from the present, either stuck in the past or worried about the future.

Gate 21—Control ○

Force of Nature, Control, Taking Charge, Managing Resources

GIFT: Natural ability to manage and control resources

HIGH EXPRESSION: Effective at taking charge and ensuring resources are used wisely. Keen sense of when to hold on and when to let go, balancing Authority with service.

LOW EXPRESSION: Becoming overly controlling or fearful of losing control. Struggling with power dynamics, either dominating or being dominated by others.

Gate 22—Grace ○

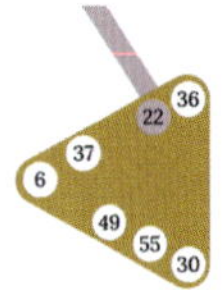

Openness, Grace and Charm, Emotional Depth, Beauty

GIFT: Embodying emotional grace and depth

HIGH EXPRESSION: Expressing emotions with elegance and authenticity; creating a sense of harmony in relationships. Bringing beauty and refinement to emotional experiences.

LOW EXPRESSION: Feeling emotionally overwhelmed or shut down. Struggling with moodiness or difficulty expressing emotions constructively.

Gate 23—Simplicity ○

Simplicity, To the Point, Powerful Words, Truth

GIFT: Talent for simplifying complex ideas

HIGH EXPRESSION: Expressing insights clearly and succinctly, making difficult concepts accessible to others. Skilled at translating abstract ideas into practical knowledge.

LOW EXPRESSION: Feeling misunderstood or struggling to communicate insights effectively. Becoming frustrated when others do not see things the same way.

Gate 24—Rationalization

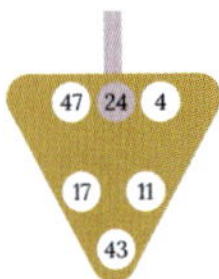

Insightfulness, Rationalization, Silence, Mental Renewal

GIFT: Ability to bring mental clarity

HIGH EXPRESSION: Finding peace in contemplation and bringing understanding to confusion. Talented at resolving mental dilemmas and finding inner quiet.

LOW EXPRESSION: Becoming stuck in mental loops or overthinking situations. Struggling with letting go of uncertainty and needing to rationalize everything.

Gate 25—Innocence

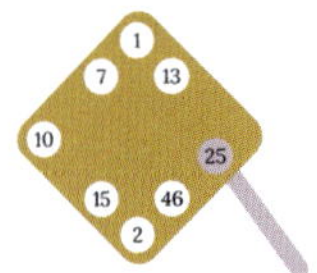

Innocence, Open-Hearted, Unconditional Love, Acceptance

GIFT: Embodying universal love and innocence

HIGH EXPRESSION: Expressing pure, unconditional love that transcends personal attachment. Capable of seeing the divine in all experiences and inspiring others to do the same.

LOW EXPRESSION: Feeling disconnected from a higher self or spiritual path. Struggling with feelings of disillusionment or spiritual crisis.

Gate 26—Persuasion

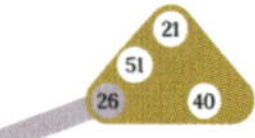

Commitment, Brighter Future, Sales, Integrity

GIFT: Skilled at influencing and persuading others

HIGH EXPRESSION: Using willpower and charm to promote and sell ideas or products with integrity. Knowing how to maximize opportunities and bring success.

LOW EXPRESSION: Resorting to manipulation or exaggeration to get one's way. Struggling with honesty and integrity in interactions.

Gate 27—Caring

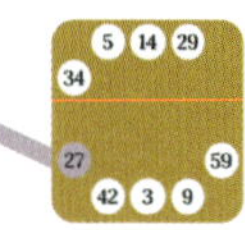

Caring, Nurturing, Nourishing, Responsibility

GIFT: Natural inclination to care for and nurture others

HIGH EXPRESSION: Protective and supportive, creating environments where others feel safe and cared for. Understanding the importance of nourishment, both physically and emotionally.

LOW EXPRESSION: Overextending oneself in caring for others, neglecting personal needs. Struggling with feeling unappreciated or overly responsible.

Gate 28—Risk-Taking

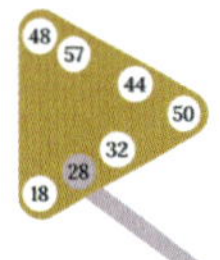

Risk Taker, Thriller, Fighter, Courage

GIFT: Finding purpose through struggle and challenge

HIGH EXPRESSION: Facing life's challenges with courage and determination, finding deeper meaning in overcoming obstacles. Inspiring others to see struggles as opportunities for growth.

LOW EXPRESSION: Feeling life is meaningless or constantly fighting against circumstances. Struggling with existential fear or feeling life is a series of battles.

Gate 29—Commitment

Devotion, Intense Joy, Tenacious

GIFT: Naturally persistent and committed

HIGH EXPRESSION: Bringing perseverance and dedication to whatever one is committed to, helping projects reach completion. Knowing how to say yes to the right opportunities with full-hearted enthusiasm.

LOW EXPRESSION: Struggling with overcommitting or committing to the wrong things. Feeling trapped or exhausted by unfulfilling commitments.

Gate 30—Desire

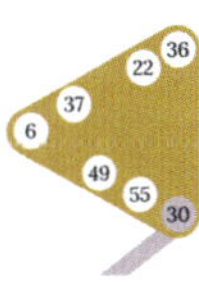

Desire to Feel and Inspire Others to Feel Deeply, Emotional Experiences, Intensity, Feelings

GIFT: Deeply passionate and driven by desires

HIGH EXPRESSION: Bringing intensity and clarity to desires, knowing how to channel emotional energy into manifestation. Helping others connect with their own passions.

LOW EXPRESSION: Feeling overwhelmed by desires or becoming fixated on unfulfilled longings. Struggling with emotional highs and lows, feeling either too much or too little.

Gate 31—Leading

Leading, Influence, Collective Vision

GIFT: Natural ability to influence others through presence and words

HIGH EXPRESSION: Leaders who inspire others to follow a vision or direction. Using influence responsibly for the benefit of the group.

LOW EXPRESSION: Struggling with feeling unheard or ineffective in leadership roles. Misusing influence, becoming authoritarian or manipulative.

Gate 32—Continuity

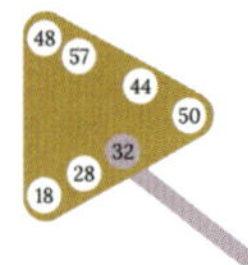

Continuity, Restraint, Highly Influential, Change, Success and Failure, Thriving, Foresight

GIFT: Adept at recognizing what has enduring value

HIGH EXPRESSION: Nurturing and sustaining what is valuable, ensuring it survives and thrives. Skilled at spotting potential and fostering it with patience and care.

LOW EXPRESSION: Feeling insecure about the future or fearing failure. Becoming overly cautious or resistant to change, missing opportunities for growth.

Gate 33—Reflection

Contemplation, Privacy, Memories, Experience, Wisdom

GIFT: Natural ability to reflect on and learn from the past

HIGH EXPRESSION: Wise historians who provide valuable insights from past experiences. Knowing when to share reflections and when to keep them private.

LOW EXPRESSION: Feeling stuck in the past or burdened by memories. Struggling with letting go of past experiences and moving forward.

Gate 34—Power

Empowerment, Steadfastness, Sovereignty, Power

GIFT: Embodying raw, innate power and strength

HIGH EXPRESSION: Acting decisively in the moment with great energy and effectiveness. Capable of achieving significant things through sheer determination and presence.

LOW EXPRESSION: Struggling with impatience or aggression, acting impulsively without consideration. Becoming overbearing or burning out from overexertion.

Gate 35—Change

Adventure, Emotional Experiences, Learning, Change

GIFT: Driven by a desire for new experiences and adventure

HIGH EXPRESSION: Bringing change and exploration, constantly seeking to expand horizons. Adaptable and inspiring others to embrace life's journey.

LOW EXPRESSION: Feeling restless or dissatisfied with the current situation. Struggling with boredom or a constant need for new stimulation.

Gate 36—Surrender ○

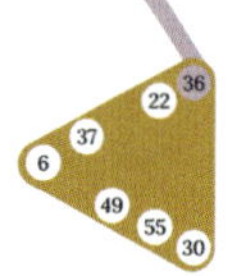

Gentleness, Emotional Wisdom, Humanity, Compassion, Crisis

GIFT: Ability to navigate emotional crises and uncertainty

HIGH EXPRESSION: Emotionally resilient and able to handle intense situations with grace. Helping others navigate difficult emotions and find maturity through challenging experiences.

LOW EXPRESSION: Feeling overwhelmed by emotional turbulence and reacting impulsively. Struggling with drama or creating crises when things feel too calm.

Gate 37—Friendship ○

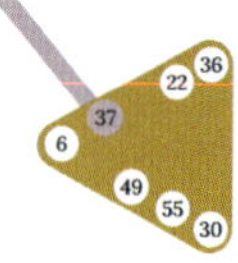

Friendship, Community, Togetherness, Equality, Emotional Resources, Holding People Together

GIFT: Naturally inclined to create harmony and community

HIGH EXPRESSION: Bringing people together and fostering close-knit bonds, creating supportive and caring environments. Valuing loyalty and cooperation, making others feel safe.

LOW EXPRESSION: Feeling isolated or struggling with conflict in relationships. Becoming overly accommodating; sacrificing personal needs for the sake of peace.

Gate 38—The Fighter ○

Fighter, Perseverance, Struggle, Discernment, Having Meaning

GIFT: Strong sense of purpose and determination

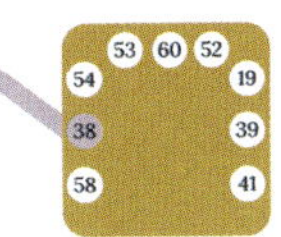

HIGH EXPRESSION: Willing to stand up for what one believes in, finding meaning through struggles. Inspiring others to fight for their values and what truly matters.

LOW EXPRESSION: Becoming combative or feeling like life is a constant battle. Struggling with finding a sense of purpose and feeling frustrated or resentful.

Gate 39—Provocation

Provocation, Clarity, Transformation, Unstuck

GIFT: Provoking growth and transformation

HIGH EXPRESSION: Challenging others to break free from stagnation and push beyond comfort zones. Acting as a catalyst for emotional and spiritual awakening.

LOW EXPRESSION: Provoking without purpose, creating unnecessary tension or conflict. Struggling with feeling misunderstood or isolated due to a provocative nature.

Gate 40—Providing

Aloneness, Boundaries, Rest, Balance, Service

GIFT: Valuing independence and self-sufficiency

HIGH EXPRESSION: Balancing work and rest, finding strength in providing for oneself and others. Appreciating alone time and recharging through solitude.

LOW EXPRESSION: Feeling isolated or overburdened by responsibilities. Struggling with asking for help or feeling undervalued for efforts.

Gate 41—Potential

Hopes and Dreams, Divine Timing, Felt Experiences, Evolution, Transformation

GIFT: A vivid imagination and the ability to dream

HIGH EXPRESSION: Initiating new cycles and stories, inspiring others to explore possibilities and create new experiences. Visionary bringing fresh ideas into reality.

LOW EXPRESSION: Feeling stuck in fantasies without manifesting them into reality. Struggling with dissatisfaction or feeling that dreams are unattainable.

Gate 42—Growth

Celebration, Closing Loops, Full Potential, Growth

GIFT: Skilled at seeing things through to the end

HIGH EXPRESSION: Bringing processes to completion, ensuring growth and learning are achieved. Understanding the importance of closing chapters to make way for new beginnings.

LOW EXPRESSION: Struggling with letting go or feeling unfulfilled by endings. Fearing moving on and becoming stuck in repetitive cycles.

Gate 43—Breakthrough

Insight, Realization, A-ha Moments, Clarity

GIFT: Deeply insightful with the ability to understand things intuitively

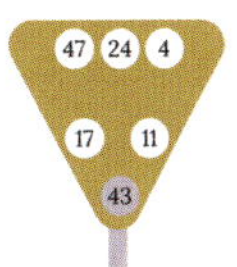

HIGH EXPRESSION: Bringing unique and transformative insights, seeing things that others cannot. Expressing ideas clearly and having a profound impact on how others perceive the world.

LOW EXPRESSION: Feeling misunderstood or unable to communicate insights effectively. Struggling with doubt and fear of rejection.

Gate 44—Breaking Patterns ○

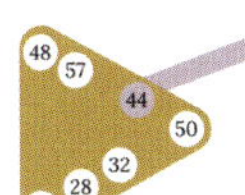

Patterns, The Past, Possibility, Transformation, Alertness

GIFT: Keen sense of pattern recognition

HIGH EXPRESSION: Seeing patterns and anticipating outcomes, helping others prepare for the future. Skilled at recognizing what needs to be repeated or avoided for success.

LOW EXPRESSION: Feeling haunted by past mistakes or becoming overly cautious. Struggling with anxiety about the future or fear of repeating the past.

Gate 45—Authority ○

Leadership, Money, Well-Being, Distribution, Gathering Resources

GIFT: Natural leaders and stewards of resources

HIGH EXPRESSION: Leading with Authority and wisdom, knowing how to manage and distribute resources for the benefit of the community. Inspiring trust and respect.

LOW EXPRESSION: Struggling with the need for control or fear of losing Authority. Becoming possessive or overly focused on material resources.

Gate 46—Embodiment

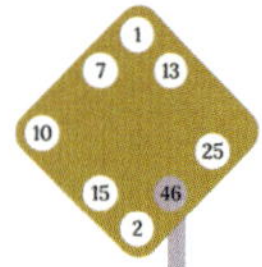

Embodiment, Bliss, Body Awareness, Love of Physical Self

GIFT: Embodying the love of life and physical existence

HIGH EXPRESSION: Grounded and fully present in the body, embracing life with joy and grace. Inspiring others to love being alive.

LOW EXPRESSION: Feeling disconnected from the body or struggling with self-worth. Neglecting well-being or feeling unlucky or undeserving of good fortune.

Gate 47—Realization

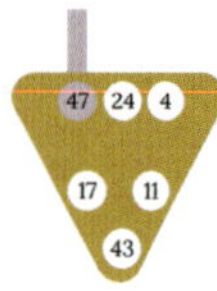

Patterns, The Past, Possibility, Transformation, Alertness

GIFT: Organizing abstract thoughts into coherent insights and realizations

HIGH EXPRESSION: Transforming mental confusion into insight and realization. Helping others see the bigger picture and find peace in uncertainty.

LOW EXPRESSION: Feeling overwhelmed by mental pressure or stuck in confusion. Struggling with self-doubt and a lack of mental clarity.

Gate 48—Depth

Depth, Wisdom, Understanding, Inadequacy

GIFT: Possessing deep wisdom and knowledge

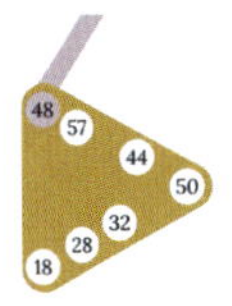

HIGH EXPRESSION: Bringing depth and understanding to any situation, knowing how to dive deep into the core of a matter. Valued as a resource for knowledge and insight.

LOW EXPRESSION: Feeling inadequate or fearing a lack of depth needed to contribute. Struggling with impostor syndrome or perfectionism.

Gate 49—Principles

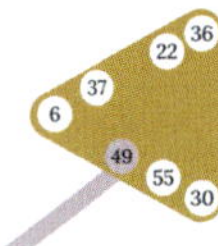

Revolution, Principles, Leading, Transformation

GIFT: Standing firmly in principles and values

HIGH EXPRESSION: Advocating for change based on what is just and fair. Acting as a catalyst for social evolution, aligning actions with core values.

LOW EXPRESSION: Becoming inflexible or overly judgmental, rejecting others who do not share beliefs. Struggling with intolerance or being too radical.

Gate 50—Values

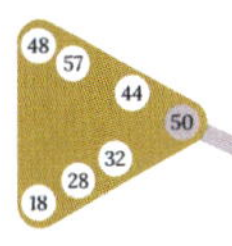

Values, Harmony, Collective Empowerment, Responsibility

GIFT: Deeply connected to responsibility and care for the tribe

HIGH EXPRESSION: Upholding values and providing guidance to maintain community well-being. Acting as a protector who creates a safe and nurturing Environment.

LOW EXPRESSION: Feeling overwhelmed by responsibilities or becoming overly controlling. Struggling with letting go or allowing others to have different values.

Gate 51—Shock

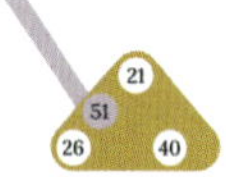

Shock, Awakening, Unconditional Love, Powerful

GIFT: Embodying courage and willingness to take risks

HIGH EXPRESSION: Bold and fearless, willing to face the unknown and shock others into growth. Acting as a catalyst for awakening and transformation.

LOW EXPRESSION: Being reckless or creating unnecessary drama. Struggling with impulsivity or needing to prove courage.

Gate 52—Stillness

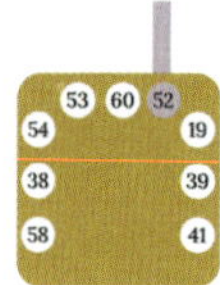

Stillness, Concentration, Steady Watching, Ebbing and Flowing, Inaction

GIFT: Bringing calm and stillness to situations

HIGH EXPRESSION: Providing focus and patience, creating stability and stillness. Acting as a grounding force, helping others find clarity in chaos.

LOW EXPRESSION: Feeling stuck or apathetic, struggling to take action. Becoming too passive or resistant to change.

Gate 53—Beginnings

Initiating, New Beginnings, Opportunities

GIFT: Skilled at initiating new beginnings

HIGH EXPRESSION: Bringing energy and enthusiasm to start new projects and cycles. Inspiring others to embrace new experiences and possibilities.

LOW EXPRESSION: Struggling with commitment or feeling overwhelmed by new starts. Leaving things unfinished or lacking the follow-through to see things through.

Gate 54—Ambition

Spiritual Growth, Ambition, Material Mastery

GIFT: Driven by ambition and the desire to rise

HIGH EXPRESSION: Motivated to achieve and elevate oneself and others. Knowing how to use drive and determination to create opportunities for success.

LOW EXPRESSION: Becoming overly focused on personal gain or status. Struggling with impatience or unethical behavior to achieve goals.

Gate 55—Abundance

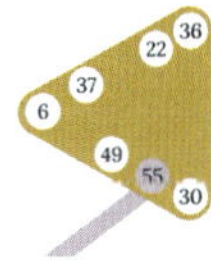

Abundance, Faith, Creativity, Finding Lightness in Darkness, Spirit

GIFT: Deeply connected to emotional freedom and spirit

HIGH EXPRESSION: Embodying emotional independence and knowing how to transform emotional experiences into wisdom. Open to the abundance of life and inspiring others to feel free.

LOW EXPRESSION: Feeling overwhelmed by emotional highs and lows or struggling with victimhood. Becoming emotionally reactive or feeling trapped by feelings.

Gate 56—Storytelling

Stimulation, Stories, Delight, Empowerment

GIFT: Being a storyteller who brings meaning through words

HIGH EXPRESSION: Sharing experiences and insights in a way that inspires and educates others. Knowing how to captivate and entertain through storytelling.

LOW EXPRESSION: Struggling with superficiality or feeling pressured to keep people interested. Becoming detached from personal experiences, telling stories without substance.

Gate 57—Intuition

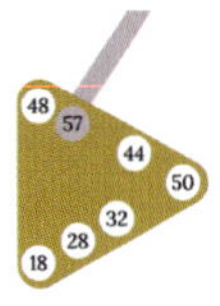

Intuition, Insights, Clarity, Trust, Knowing

GIFT: Possessing deep intuitive awareness

HIGH EXPRESSION: Highly intuitive and able to pick up on subtle energies. Bringing clarity and insight to situations, helping others make wise decisions.

LOW EXPRESSION: Struggling with fear or doubt, ignoring intuitive hits. Becoming overly anxious or disconnected from inner knowing.

Gate 58—Vitality

Aliveness, Joy, Vitality, Potential, Transformation

GIFT: Driven by a love for improvement and vitality

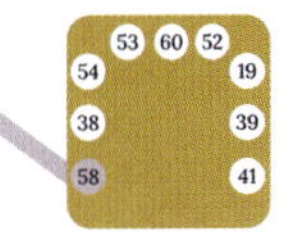

HIGH EXPRESSION: Bringing enthusiasm and joy to the process of growth and betterment. Inspiring others to strive for excellence and find joy in continuous improvement.

LOW EXPRESSION: Becoming overly critical or dissatisfied, focusing on what's wrong rather than what's right. Struggling with a lack of joy and contentment.

Gate 59—Intimacy

Intimacy, Sexuality, Vulnerability, Honesty

GIFT: Naturally gifted in creating intimacy and bonds

HIGH EXPRESSION: Breaking down barriers and creating deep connections with others. Warm and approachable, fostering trust and closeness.

LOW EXPRESSION: Feeling isolated or struggling with vulnerability. Creating distance or feeling uncomfortable with intimacy.

Gate 60—Acceptance

Limitation, Magic, Embodied, Laws of Nature, Acceptance

GIFT: Adept at accepting limitations and embracing possibilities

HIGH EXPRESSION: Knowing how to work within constraints and find creative solutions. Embracing life's limitations and using them as a foundation for growth and innovation.

LOW EXPRESSION: Feeling restricted or frustrated by limitations, becoming pessimistic or resentful. Struggling with rigidity or resistance to change.

Gate 61—Inner Knowing ○

Mystery, Inner Knowing, Truth, Mystic

GIFT: Connected to the mysteries of life and deep contemplation

HIGH EXPRESSION: Bringing a sense of wonder and curiosity, seeking deeper understanding of life's mysteries. Insightful and bringing profound clarity to abstract concepts.

LOW EXPRESSION: Struggling with mental anxiety or obsession with finding the truth. Becoming disconnected from reality, lost in abstract thinking.

Gate 62—Details ○

Details, Piercing Language, Clarity, Translation, Organization

GIFT: Highly detailed and skilled at communication

HIGH EXPRESSION: Bringing precision and clarity to communication, helping others understand complex ideas. Methodical and practical in approach.

LOW EXPRESSION: Becoming overly focused on details, missing the bigger picture. Struggling with perfectionism or feeling overwhelmed by minor issues.

Gate 63—Questioning ○

Doubt, Discernment, Potential, Questioner, Needing Answers

GIFT: Bringing a healthy skepticism and the drive for clarity

HIGH EXPRESSION: Asking the right questions and challenging assumptions, fostering growth and understanding. Bringing thoughtful analysis and critical thinking to problem-solving.

LOW EXPRESSION: Struggling with self-doubt or excessive questioning. Becoming paralyzed by uncertainty or unable to trust personal judgment.

Gate 64—Confusion

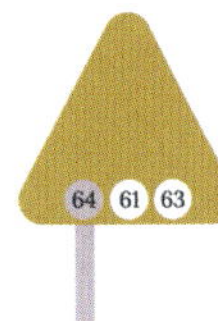

Imagination, Confusion, Illumination, Creativity

GIFT: Harnessing the chaos of confusion to inspire new perspectives and possibilities

HIGH EXPRESSION: Adept at processing complex information and making sense of confusion. Helping others find clarity and peace in uncertainty.

LOW EXPRESSION: Feeling overwhelmed by mental pressure or getting lost in confusion. Struggling with decision-making or fear of making mistakes.

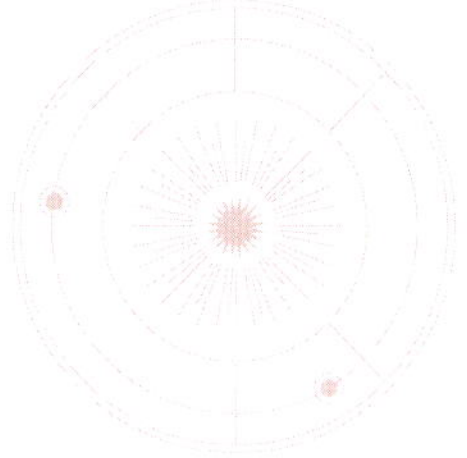

Reflection

☉ **SUN:** My core energy and personal power is in

Gate ______, which represents ______________________________ and in

Gate ______, which represents ______________________________.

⊕ **EARTH:** What grounds me and brings me stability is in

Gate ______, which represents ______________________________ and in

Gate ______, which represents ______________________________.

☊ **NORTH NODE:** The direction I'm headed and wisdom of my future is in Gate ______, which represents ______________________________

and in Gate ______, which represents ______________________________.

☋ **SOUTH NODE:** My past life energy and the energy I'm moving away from is in Gate ______, which represents ______________________________

and in Gate ______, which represents ______________________________.

☽ **MOON:** What drives me in life is in

Gate ______, which represents ______________________________ and in

Gate ______, which represents ______________________________.

☿ **MERCURY:** What I'm here to communicate and share is in

Gate ______, which represents ______________________________ and in

Gate ______, which represents ______________________________.

♀ **VENUS:** What I morally value and love is in Gate ______, which represents ______ and in Gate ______, which represents ______.

♂ **MARS:** Where I have the chance to mature is in Gate ______, which represents ______ and in Gate ______, which represents ______.

♃ **JUPITER:** Where I can lean in to find rewards is in Gate ______, which represents ______ and in Gate ______, which represents ______.

♄ **SATURN:** Where I'm learning to take responsibility for my behavior is in Gate ______, which represents ______ and in Gate ______, which represents ______.

♅ **URANUS:** Where I deviate from the norm and am different is in Gate ______, which represents ______ and in Gate ______, which represents ______.

♆ **NEPTUNE:** Where my spiritual work is and what brings me joy is in Gate ______, which represents ______ and in Gate ______, which represents ______.

♇ **PLUTO:** My truth and shadow work for inner transformation is in Gate ______, which represents ______ and in Gate ______, which represents ______.

⚷ **CHIRON:** Where I heal and transform my deepest wounds is in Gate ______, which represents ______ and in Gate ______, which represents ______.

CHANNELS: YOUR CONSISTENT AND STRONG GIFTS

Channels are where you hold your strongest and most consistent gifts. They represent the pathways that connect two Gates together, forming a line of energy between two colored-in Energy Centers in your chart. When a Channel is defined, it amplifies the energy of the two Gates it connects and creates a consistent flow of energy in your life.

Think of Channels as bridges. Just as a bridge connects two distinct pieces of land, each Channel forms a direct link between two Gates on your chart. This connection allows for a seamless and amplified flow of energy, blending the qualities of each Gate. While Gates represent individual gifts, Channels bridge these aspects together, creating an even more powerful and unified expression of your gifts. So you can think of your Channels as your core gifts or strengths.

You can identify Channels in your BodyGraph as the lines that connect two Energy Centers. There are thirty-six Channels in total, and your chart will have anywhere from zero to ten activated Channels. How many Channels you have will influence how focused or spread out your gifts are:

- With fewer Channels, your gifts may feel more concentrated in specific areas.
- With more Channels, your gifts may feel broader, creating a dynamic flow between multiple Centers.
- With zero Channels, this means you're a Reflector Energy Type, as Reflectors have no Defined Centers or Channels in their chart.

Instead of relying on consistent energy flow within themselves, Reflectors take in and amplify the energy of the people and environments around them, feeling everyone's gifts.

Note: Your Channels will be also listed when you look up your chart. We have included a circle beside each Channel for you to check whether you have it or not.

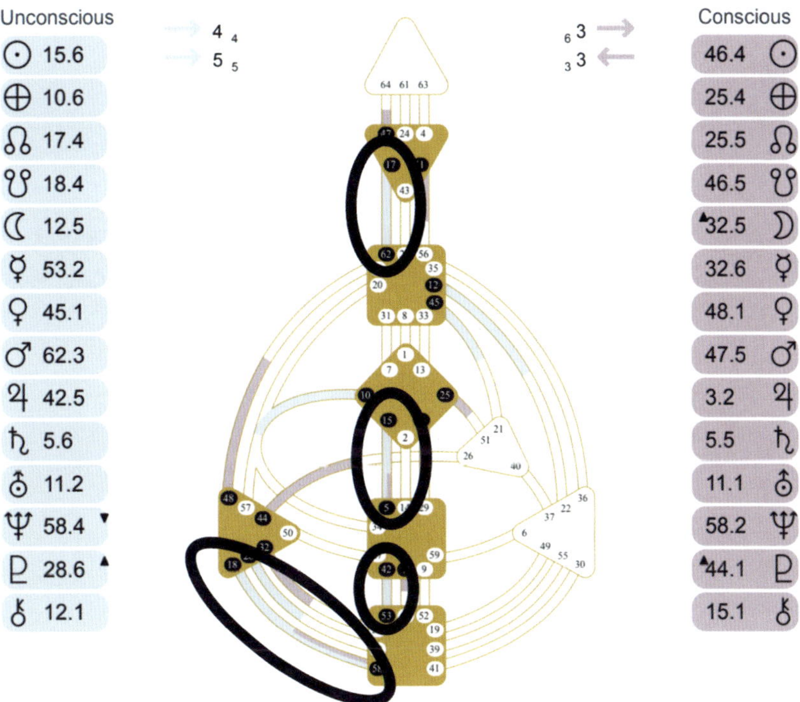

Channel of Abstraction (64–47) ○

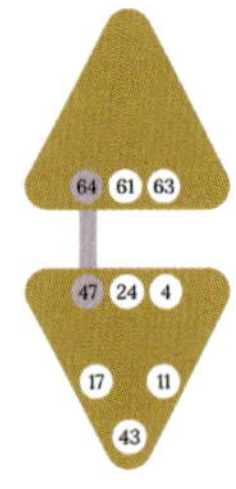

Abstract Thinking, Confusion, Processing, Reflection, Clarity

This Channel connects Gate 64 (Confusion) and Gate 47 (Realization), allowing individuals to process confusing, abstract experiences and bring clarity to past events.

The Core Gift of this Channel is the ability to take abstract, nonlinear experiences and make sense of them, primarily for the benefit of others.

TIPS FOR THIS CHANNEL:

- Be comfortable with confusion, as it is part of your process.
- Use visual tools to process and understand the past.

Channel of Awareness (61–24) ○

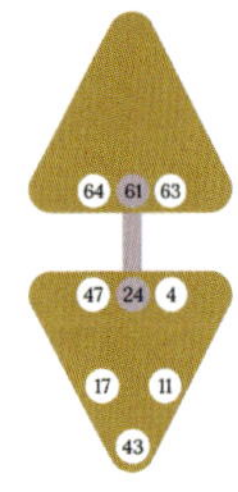

Inner Knowing, Mysteries, Insights, Enlightenment, Inspiration

This Channel connects Gate 61 (Inner Knowing) and Gate 24 (Rationalization), creating a strong ability to think deeply and bring awareness to life's mysteries. It seeks to inspire new ways of thinking and uncover hidden truths.

The Core Gift of this Channel is the ability to access inner knowing and psychic-like awareness, offering insights that enlighten others.

TIPS FOR THIS CHANNEL:

- Give yourself time for insights to develop.
- Wait for the right moment to share your insights with others.

Channel of Logic (63–4)

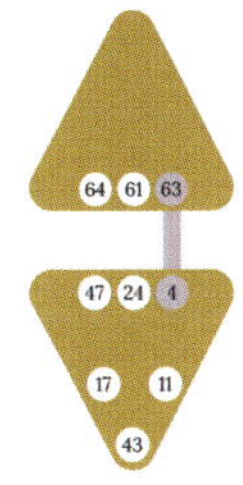

Doubt, Solutions, Mental Clarity, Rational Thinking, Investigation

This Channel connects Gate 63 (Questioning) and Gate 4 (Understanding), creating a strong logical mind that questions and analyzes patterns to bring truths to light. The energy here seeks to resolve doubt by finding clear, logical answers.

The Core Gift of this Channel is the ability to question and challenge assumptions to find clarity and truth, often helping others see things from a new perspective.

TIPS FOR THIS CHANNEL:

- Don't use logic to place yourself on a pedestal.
- Make sure you have a healthy amount of skepticism, but not so much that you doubt everything.

Channel of Acceptance (17–62)

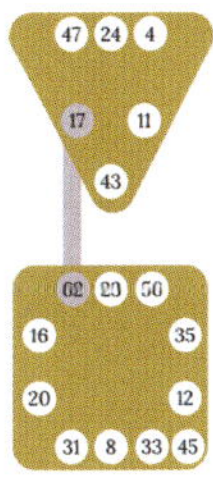

Logic, Structure, Organization, Big Picture, Detail-Oriented

This Channel connects Gate 17 (Solutions) and Gate 62 (Details), giving individuals the ability to organize and make sense of details, seeing how they fit into a larger structure.

The Core Gift of this Channel is the ability to organize and translate complex details into an understandable big picture for others.

TIPS FOR THIS CHANNEL:

- Wait for the right audience before sharing your organizational insights.
- Use your gift of organization to serve your community.

Channel of Insights (43–23) ○

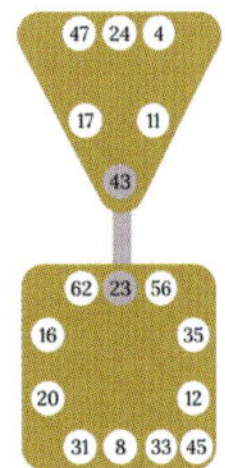

Genius, Innovation, Individuality, Expression, Breakthrough

This Channel connects Gate 43 (Breakthroughs) and Gate 23 (Simplicity), emphasizing the process of transforming unique insights into understandable concepts. It's often referred to as the Channel of "Genius to Freak," highlighting the fine line between revolutionary ideas and their perception by others.

The Core Gift of this Channel is the ability to conceptualize and communicate breakthrough ideas that can change the way people think or live.

TIPS FOR THIS CHANNEL:

- Trust your insights even if they are initially met with resistance.
- Find effective ways to communicate your ideas so they can be more easily understood by others.

Channel of Curiosity (11–56) ○

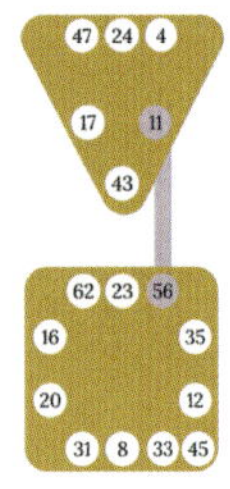

Inspiration, Ideas, Storytelling, Exploration, Learning

This Channel connects Gate 11 (Ideas) and Gate 56 (Storytelling), leading to an insatiable curiosity and a love for gathering and sharing stories, ideas, and inspiration with others.

The Core Gift of this Channel is the ability to inspire others through storytelling and sharing the lessons learned from your curiosity.

TIPS FOR THIS CHANNEL:

- Avoid pressuring yourself to chase every idea.
- Wait to be invited before sharing your stories or insights.

Channel of Talent (48–16) ○

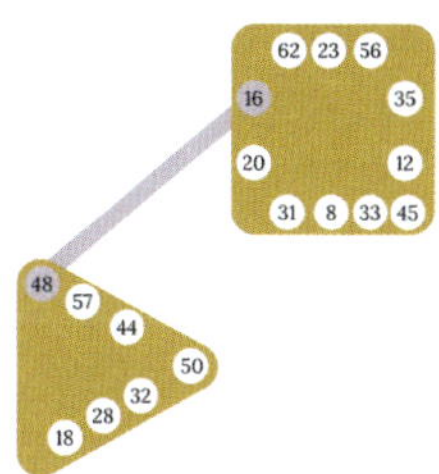

Mastery, Skill, Depth, Wisdom, Performance

This Channel connects Gate 48 (Depth) and Gate 16 (Skills), leading to a profound ability to develop talent through wisdom and experience, often becoming a master in your chosen field.

The Core Gift of this Channel is the ability to bring deep mastery and skill to any endeavor, driven by a desire to excel and be recognized for your talents.

TIPS FOR THIS CHANNEL:

- Know that you are enough and more talented than you may realize.
- Embrace your expertise and feel proud of your abilities.

Channel of Spontaneity (57–20) ○

Instinct, Presence, Intuition, Spontaneous Expression

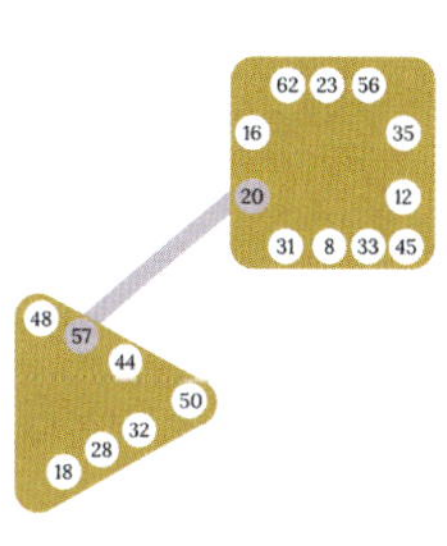

This Channel connects Gate 57 (Intuition) and Gate 20 (Presence), creating an ability to see what is happening before others are made aware. It connects intuition directly to voice, allowing for spontaneous and insightful expression.

The Core Gift of this Channel is the ability to act on intuitive insights instantly, often knowing what needs to be said or done in the moment.

TIPS FOR THIS CHANNEL:

- Ensure your audience is receptive before sharing spontaneous insights.
- Don't let fears about the future drown out your intuitive whispers.

Channel of Self-Love (10–20) ○

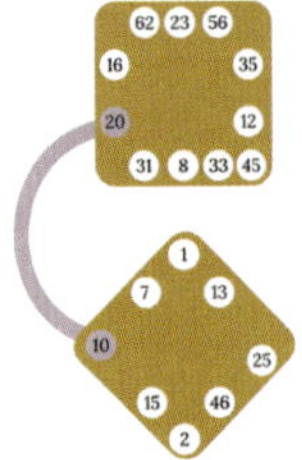

Authenticity, Self-Love, Empowerment, Presence, Expression

This Channel connects Gate 10 (Self-Love) and Gate 20 (Presence), fostering a gift for expressing oneself authentically in the present moment. This authenticity inspires others to love themselves and step into their truth.

The Core Gift of this Channel is the ability to inspire self-love and authenticity in others, showing them how to live life in alignment with their true selves.

TIPS FOR THIS CHANNEL:

- Wait to share your voice with those who invite your energy in.
- Surround yourself with people who value your authentic self.

Channel of Leadership (7–31) ○

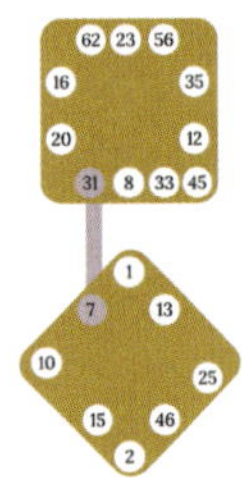

Influence, Humility, Leadership, Guidance, Trust

This Channel connects Gate 7 (The Leader) and Gate 31 (Leading), enabling a humble and trustworthy leadership style. You may naturally find yourself in leadership positions without seeking them out.

The Core Gift of this Channel is the ability to lead others with humility and integrity, earning their trust and guiding them toward their goals.

TIPS FOR THIS CHANNEL:

- Embrace your leadership role and know the influence you have on others.
- Recognize that you can lead without dictating or controlling.

Channel of Creativity (1–8)

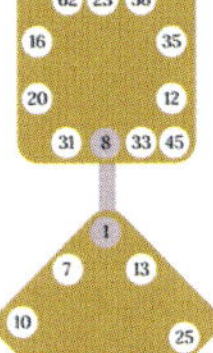

Creativity, Innovation, Expression, Contribution, Boldness

This Channel connects Gate 1 (Creativity) and Gate 8 (Contribution), creating a powerful force for creative self-expression. It drives individuals to contribute their unique talents and inspire others through their bold creative pursuits.

The Core Gift of this Channel is the ability to channel creative inspiration into something that inspires and uplifts others, encouraging them to express their uniqueness.

TIPS FOR THIS CHANNEL:

- Express yourself boldly without fear of rejection.
- Embrace your authenticity to magnetize the right people and opportunities.

Channel of Listening (13–33)

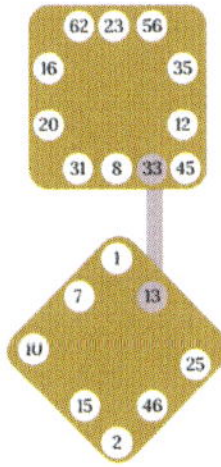

Listening, Reflection, Wisdom, Secrets, Trust

This Channel connects Gate 13 (Listening) and Gate 33 (Reflection), giving you the ability to listen attentively and gather wisdom from the stories and experiences of others. You are often seen as someone whom people confide in.

The Core Gift of this Channel is the ability to hold space for others, reflect on their stories, and provide wisdom that prevents the repetition of mistakes.

TIPS FOR THIS CHANNEL:

- Pause before sharing your wisdom to ensure others are ready to hear it.
- Find a balance between withholding and sharing your insights.

Channel of Charisma (34–20) ○

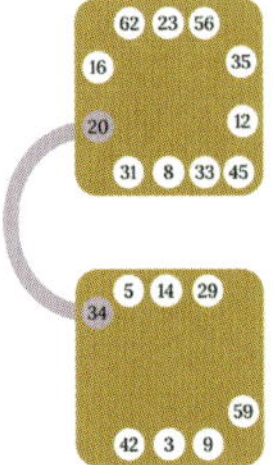

Manifestation, Power, Presence, Creative Flow, Life Force

This Channel connects Gate 34 (Power) and Gate 20 (Presence), creating a powerful and charismatic energy that allows you to manifest things quickly and bring life to your ideas. It represents the essence of Manifesting Generator energy.

The Core Gift of this Channel is the ability to bring creativity and life force into the present moment, inspiring others with your energy and enthusiasm.

TIPS FOR THIS CHANNEL:

- Allow yourself the space to fully express your power and charisma.
- Interact with others by responding to questions or options to activate your creative flow.

Channel of Exploration (34–10) ○

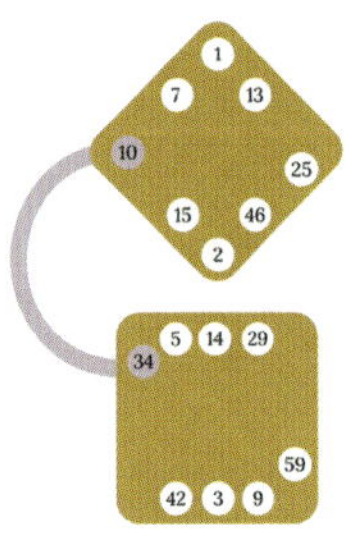

Self-Expression, Conviction, Exploration, Power, Empowerment

This Channel connects Gate 34 (Power) and Gate 10 (Self-Love), enabling you to unapologetically follow your gut and empower others with your conviction. You are meant to explore life based on your inner truth and express yourself fully.

The Core Gift of this Channel is the ability to empower others to embrace their convictions and explore their paths with confidence.

TIPS FOR THIS CHANNEL:

- Trust your gut, even when it doesn't make sense to others.
- Release any pressure to fit in, as you are meant to stand out.

Channel of Rhythm (5–15)

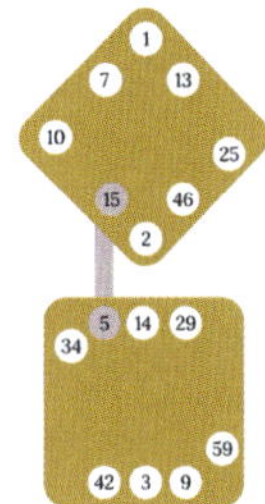

Flow, Timing, Balance, Extremes, Natural Cycles

This Channel connects Gate 5 (Rhythm) and Gate 15 (Extremes), creating a unique ability to find balance and rhythm in life. You move through life in a natural flow that may not adhere to conventional routines.

The Core Gift of this Channel is the ability to help others find their own rhythm by modeling a life of balance and natural flow.

TIPS FOR THIS CHANNEL:

- Honor your unique rhythm, even if it doesn't match societal expectations.
- Tune in to your natural cycles to return to flow when you feel rushed or out of alignment.

Channel of the Visionary (14–2)

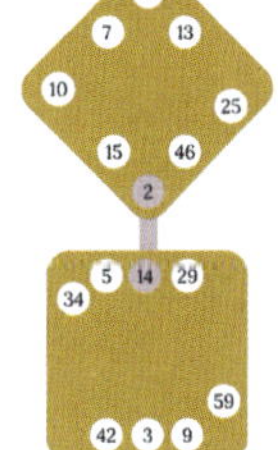

Vision, Prosperity, Direction, Manifestation, Guidance

This Channel connects Gate 14 (Prosperity) and Gate 2 (Vision), giving you the power to guide yourself and others toward their true purpose and manifest prosperity along the way. You are a visionary who paves the way for new directions in life.

The Core Gift of this Channel is the ability to trust your gut and manifest resources and support for your vision, inspiring others to follow their own paths.

TIPS FOR THIS CHANNEL:

- Trust your unique vision and gut to show you the way.
- Lead others by example, allowing them to follow their paths while you follow yours.

Channel of Discovery (29–46)

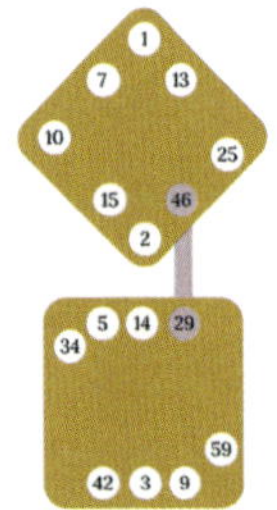

Commitment, Growth, Discovery, Life Experiences, Immersion

This Channel connects Gate 29 (Commitment) and Gate 46 (Embodiment), driving you to immerse yourself fully in life experiences and discover valuable lessons through your commitment. You have the stamina to commit deeply to what excites you.

The Core Gift of this Channel is the ability to discover new insights through life experiences and share those lessons with others, helping them grow.

TIPS FOR THIS CHANNEL:

- Use your gut to guide which experiences are worth committing to.
- Ensure your commitments honor your loyalty and dependability.

Channel of Beauty (57–10)

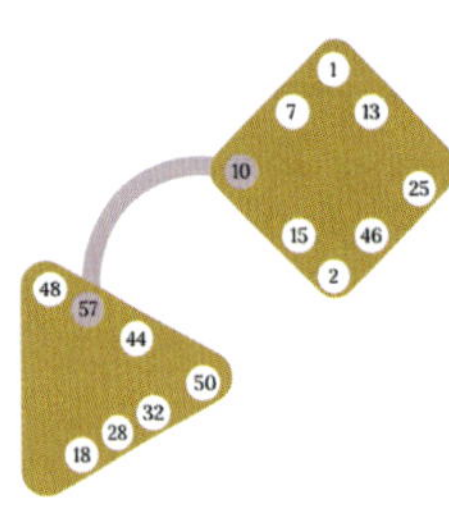

Intuition, Self-Love, Beauty, Alignment, Refinement

This Channel connects Gate 57 (Intuition) and Gate 10 (Self-Love), giving you the ability to create beauty in the world through alignment with your intuition and self-love. You refine and enhance your surroundings based on your inner knowing.

The Core Gift of this Channel is the ability to intuitively create beauty and alignment in both yourself and your environment, inspiring others to do the same.

TIPS FOR THIS CHANNEL:

- Trust your intuition to guide you toward beauty and refinement.
- Love yourself and watch it inspire the world.

Channel of Power (34–57)

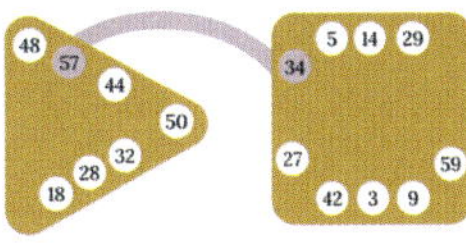

Instinct, Power, Problem-Solving, Crisis Navigation

This Channel connects Gate 34 (Power) and Gate 57 (Intuition), creating a powerful connection between your instincts and your ability to navigate challenges. You are incredibly adept at using your gut to figure out solutions to problems, even in chaotic situations.

The Core Gift of this Channel is the ability to remain calm in crises and instinctively know how to solve problems using your gut and intuition.

TIPS FOR THIS CHANNEL:

- Trust your gut instincts, especially in challenging situations.
- Strengthen your relationship with your intuition by acting on it regularly.

Channel of Nurturing (27–50)

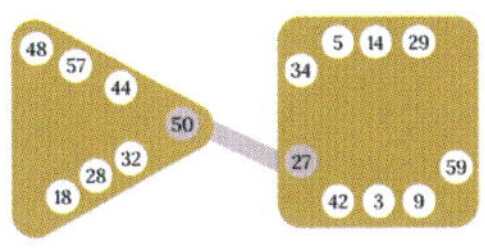

Caring, Values, Nurturing, Support, Community

This Channel connects Gate 27 (Caring) and Gate 50 (Values), giving you a natural ability to care for and nurture others, especially within a community or family context. You are deeply attuned to the needs of others and are often a source of support.

The Core Gift of this Channel is the ability to nurture and provide care for others while maintaining strong values that guide your actions.

TIPS FOR THIS CHANNEL:

- Take care of yourself before taking care of others.
- Avoid becoming over-responsible for others and allow them to grow.

Channel of Ambition (54–32)

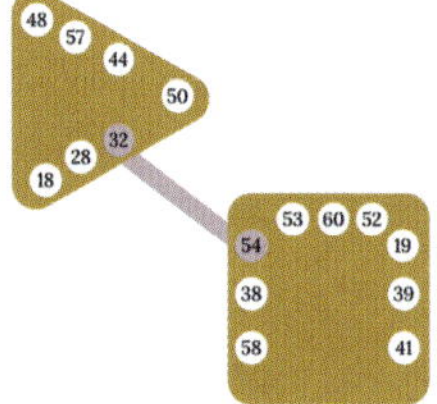

Ambition, Drive, Success, Manifestation, Determination

This Channel connects Gate 54 (Ambition) and Gate 32 (Continuity), creating a powerful drive to succeed and achieve. You are highly motivated to manifest your dreams, often working hard to achieve success and prosperity.

The Core Gift of this Channel is the ability to use your ambition and drive to manifest success and inspire others to pursue their goals.

TIPS FOR THIS CHANNEL:

- Balance ambition with self-care to avoid burnout.
- Seek support from others rather than trying to achieve everything on your own.

Channel of Tenacity (28–38)

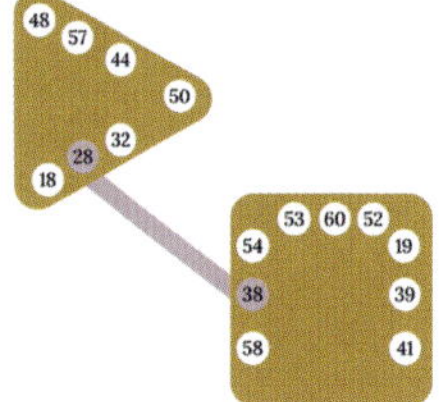

Risk-Taking, The Fighter, Struggles, Purpose, Challenges

This Channel connects Gate 28 (Risk-Taking) and Gate 38 (The Fighter), driving you to face challenges head-on and fight for what you believe in. You are naturally tenacious, and through struggles, you uncover deeper purpose in life.

The Core Gift of this Channel is the ability to empower others through your resilience and determination, showing that struggles lead to growth and purpose.

TIPS FOR THIS CHANNEL:

- Choose your battles wisely, using your intuition to guide you.
- Understand that struggles are part of your journey to finding deeper meaning.

Channel of Perfecting (18–58) ○

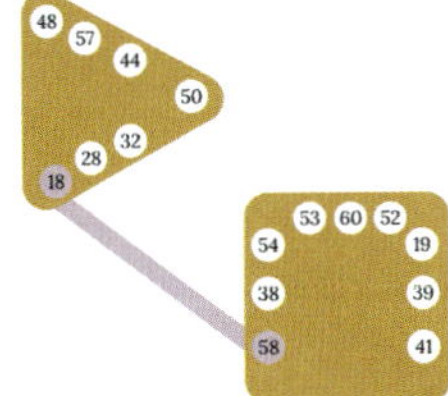

Correcting, Vitality, Improvement, Health, Mastery

This Channel connects Gate 18 (Correcting) and Gate 58 (Vitality), giving you the ability to spot what needs improvement and work to perfect it. You bring vitality to everything you do by seeking constant improvement and refinement.

The Core Gift of this Channel is the ability to bring energy and vitality into situations by offering corrections and improvements that lead to mastery.

TIPS FOR THIS CHANNEL:

- Wait for others to invite your critical eye before offering improvements.
- Focus on the process of perfecting rather than seeking unattainable perfection.

Channel of Maturation (53–42) ○

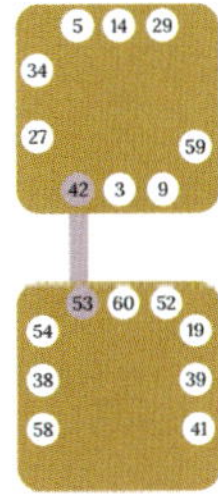

Beginnings, Growth, Cycles, Reflection, Completion

This Channel connects Gate 53 (Beginnings) and Gate 42 (Growth), making you highly attuned to the cycles of life. You are meant to initiate new experiences and see them through to completion, learning and growing along the way.

The Core Gift of this Channel is the ability to navigate life's cycles, initiate new projects, and guide them toward successful completion while reflecting on the lessons learned.

TIPS FOR THIS CHANNEL:

- Ensure that you are entering experiences that align with your purpose.
- Let go of cycles that no longer serve you and embrace new beginnings.

Channel of Innovation (60–3)

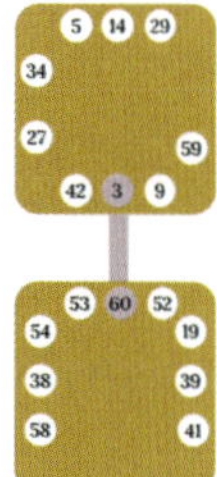

Acceptance, Order, Mutation, Transformation, New Possibilities

This Channel connects Gate 60 (Acceptance) and Gate 3 (Order), creating a natural inclination toward transformation and innovation. You go through periods of great momentum, where you create new possibilities and bring order to chaos.

The Core Gift of this Channel is the ability to embrace mutation and transformation, making way for innovative solutions and new ways of being.

TIPS FOR THIS CHANNEL:

- Embrace moments of stillness and trust that transformation is on its way.
- Allow innovation to emerge from chaos and bring order to new possibilities.

Channel of Determination (9–52)

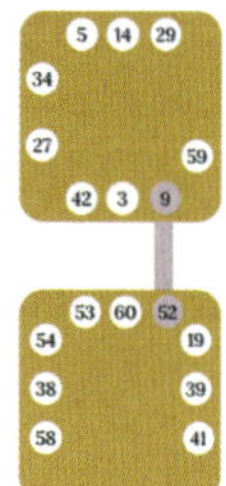

Focus, Stillness, Concentration, Discipline, Groundedness

This Channel connects Gate 9 (Focus) and Gate 52 (Stillness), giving you the ability to focus intently and concentrate on tasks, bringing a sense of discipline and groundedness to your work. You have a step-by-step approach to life that brings clarity and precision.

The Core Gift of this Channel is the ability to concentrate deeply, stay focused on the details, and bring a sense of stillness and discipline to any situation.

TIPS FOR THIS CHANNEL:

- Honor your need for focus and avoid multitasking when possible.
- Allow yourself to rest when you feel restless or unfocused.

Channel of Sensitivity (19–49)

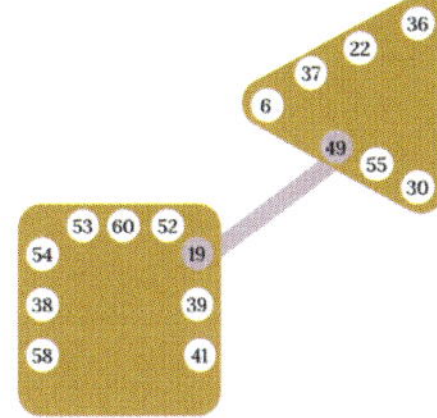

Sensitivity, Principles, Intuition, Needs, Values

This Channel connects Gate 19 (Sensitivity) and Gate 49 (Principles), giving you an innate sensitivity to the needs of others. You are deeply attuned to emotional and physical needs, and you work to align yourself and others with values that honor these needs.

The Core Gift of this Channel is the ability to sense what others need before they know it and provide nurturing care while maintaining strong principles.

TIPS FOR THIS CHANNEL:

- Balance your own needs with those of others to avoid burnout.
- Make sure your relationships align with your values.

Channel of Emoting (39–55)

Provocation, Abundance, Emotional Depth, Creativity, Moodiness

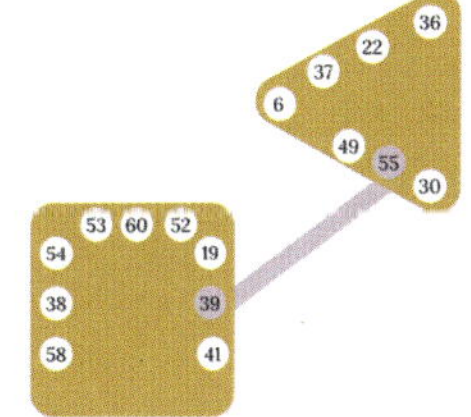

This Channel connects Gate 39 (Provocation) and Gate 55 (Abundance), giving you deep emotional sensitivity and creativity. Your emotional depth fuels your creative expression, and your moods often inspire you to channel emotions into art or other forms of expression.

The Core Gift of this Channel is the ability to provoke emotional depth in others and use your own emotional experiences to inspire creative and abundant expression.

TIPS FOR THIS CHANNEL:

- Channel your emotions into creative outlets.
- Feel it fully—loud, messy, raw, and beautifully human.

Channel of Potential (41–30)

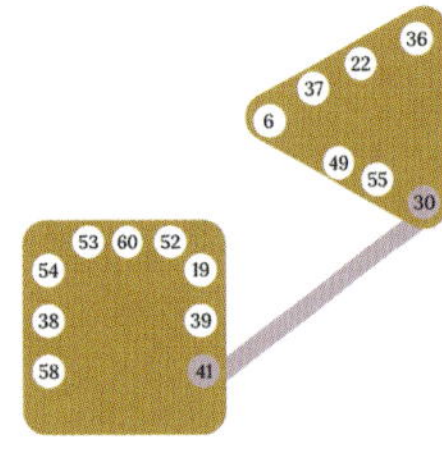

Potential, Desire, Imagination, Creative Drive, Inspiration

This Channel connects Gate 41 (Potential) and Gate 30 (Desire), giving you a strong sense of imagination and potential. You see what is possible in any situation and are driven to manifest your desires through creative expression.

The Core Gift of this Channel is the ability to see potential where others don't and inspire others to pursue their dreams and desires.

TIPS FOR THIS CHANNEL:

- Wait for clarity before pursuing your dreams, ensuring that they align with your true desires.
- Use your creative drive to inspire others to see their own potential.

Channel of Intimacy (59–6)

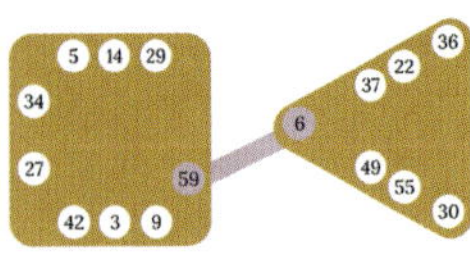

Intimacy, Discernment, Connection, Relationships, Bonding

This Channel connects Gate 59 (Intimacy) and Gate 6 (Discernment), giving you a natural ability to create close connections and bonds with others. You are skilled at fostering intimacy and deep relationships, whether in friendships, family, or romantic connections.

The Core Gift of this Channel is the ability to create meaningful and intimate connections, and even produce children or businesses.

TIPS FOR THIS CHANNEL:

- Give yourself time to develop close relationships.
- Channel your desire to create life into projects.

Channel of Community (37–40) ○

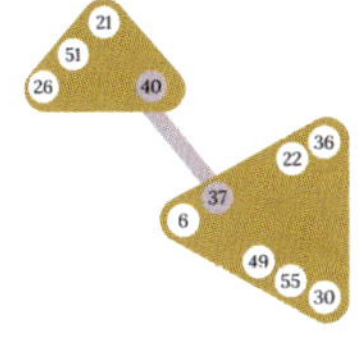

Friendship, Providing, Community, Support, Bonding

This Channel connects Gate 37 (Friendship) and Gate 40 (Providing), giving you a strong sense of community and a desire to bring people together. You are a natural provider, often seeking to support your community and create bonds of friendship and trust.

The Core Gift of this Channel is the ability to foster strong, supportive communities, bringing people together through friendship and shared values.

TIPS FOR THIS CHANNEL:

- Ensure that you feel appreciated and supported within your community.
- Invest in relationships that reciprocate the energy you put in.

Channel of Openness (12–22) ○

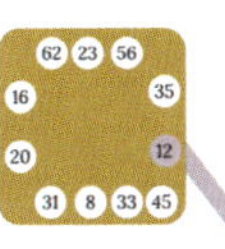

Articulation, Grace, Expression, Emotional Honesty, Performance

This Channel connects Gate 12 (Articulation) and Gate 22 (Grace), allowing you to express your emotions openly and honestly. You are skilled at using your voice to convey your feelings, whether through speech, art, or performance.

The Core Gift of this Channel is the ability to articulate emotions and inspire others to embrace their emotional honesty and expression.

TIPS FOR THIS CHANNEL:

- Pause before expressing your emotions to ensure clarity and grace in your delivery.
- Recognize the power of your voice and its impact on others.

Channel of Presence (36–35)

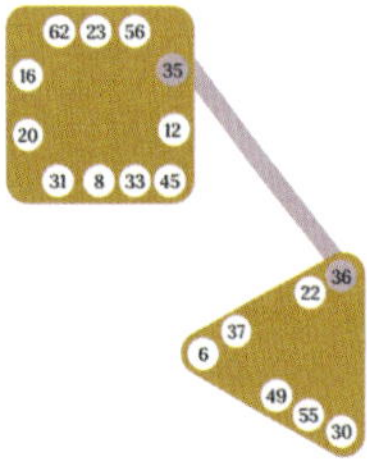

Surrender, Change, Experience, Growth, Emotional Wisdom

This Channel connects Gate 36 (Surrender) and Gate 35 (Change), giving you a strong desire for new experiences and growth. You seek to transcend limitations and embrace change, using your emotional wisdom to inspire others to take bold leaps.

The Core Gift of this Channel is the ability to inspire others to seek out new adventures and experiences, using your presence and emotional depth to guide them.

TIPS FOR THIS CHANNEL:

- Ensure that you are entering experiences that foster growth and wisdom, rather than repeating old patterns.
- Use your stories to help others face the unknown.

Channel of Marketing (44–26)

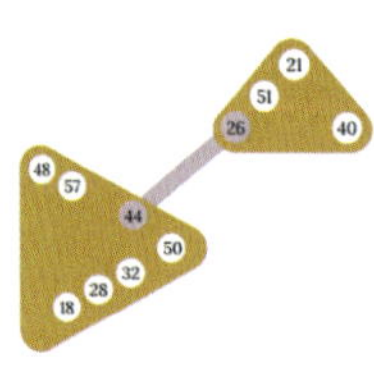

Breaking Patterns, Persuasion, Influence, Efficiency, Messaging

This Channel connects Gate 44 (Breaking Patterns) and Gate 26 (Persuasion), giving you a natural ability to influence others and create powerful, persuasive messages. You are skilled at identifying what others need and aligning them with opportunities for growth and improvement.

The Core Gift of this Channel is the ability to use your influence and marketing skills to create impactful messaging and help others improve their lives.

TIPS FOR THIS CHANNEL:

- Use your persuasive abilities for the benefit of others, not just personal gain.
- Take breaks and rest, even when your natural efficiency keeps you going.

Channel of Competitiveness (51–25) ○

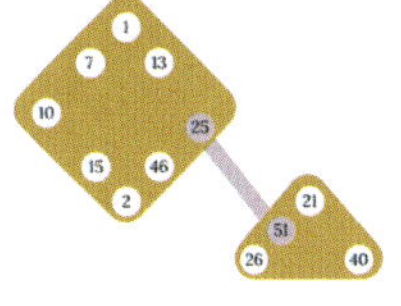

Shock, Innocence, Courage, Transformation, Competition

This Channel connects Gate 51 (Shock) and Gate 25 (Innocence), driving you to approach life with courage and a desire to overcome challenges. You are highly competitive and thrive in situations where you can push yourself to new heights, transforming yourself and others in the process.

The Core Gift of this Channel is the ability to use your competitive nature to drive transformation and inspire others to embrace their courage.

TIPS FOR THIS CHANNEL:

- Channel your competitiveness toward personal growth and improving the world.
- Avoid letting competition create unnecessary conflict in relationships.

Channel of Management (21–45) ○

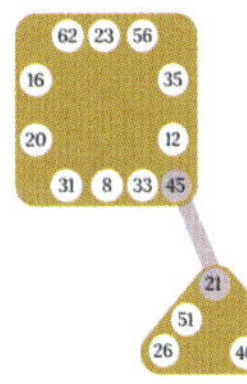

Control, Authority, Leadership, Abundance, Resources

This Channel connects Gate 21 (Control) and Gate 45 (Authority), giving you a natural sense of leadership and the ability to manage people and resources effectively. You are skilled at guiding others and creating abundance through your strategic thinking and control.

The Core Gift of this Channel is the ability to manage resources and people in a way that creates prosperity and abundance for yourself and those you lead.

TIPS FOR THIS CHANNEL:

- Learn to delegate and trust others rather than micromanaging.
- Empower others and watch your leadership multiply."

"Every one of us was born with a unique life theme that tells us what our greatest gift is, what grounds us, and how to express our purpose."

CHAPTER 9

Your LIFE THEME *and* PURPOSE

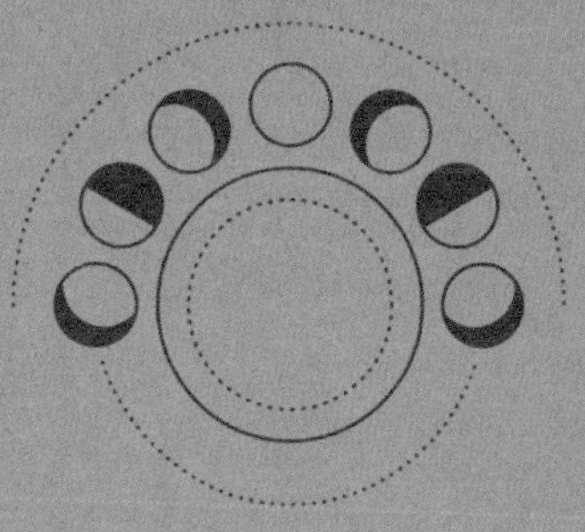

Every one of us was born with a unique life theme called your Incarnation Cross. It tells us what our greatest gift is, what grounds us, and how to express our purpose. Your Incarnation Cross doesn't involve a specific job title, relationship status, or role (e.g., "You're meant to be a doctor or a parent"). Instead, it's the central thread that weaves all parts of your design into one singular theme that frequently shows up in your life.

Think of it as the **why** behind everything in your design. Here is how it differs from other parts of your chart:

Energy Type is the **what**. It's the foundation of your chart, describing how your energy operates and interacts with the world through your Strategy.

Your Strategy is the **how**. It shows you the best way to engage with life. In other words, this is your role in life—whether a *Manifestor, Generator, Manifesting Generator, Projector*, or *Reflector*—and tells you whether you are here to **initiate**, **build**, **optimize**, **guide**, or **mirror**.

Authority is your inner **decision maker**. It helps you know what's right for you in your intuition to make the right decisions.

Profile is the **who**. It reveals the character or personality you bring to your role.

Incarnation Cross is the **why**. It's the overarching purpose that ties everything else together, providing context for your gifts and themes. Think of it like a plotline or story arc that unfolds as you move through life. It's the overarching theme that weaves through your experiences, shaped by your Energy Type, Authority, Profile, and the specific Gate gifts you carry.

While each part of your chart is important and works together, the Incarnation Cross is one of the most profound aspects. When you live in alignment with your design, you'll notice this theme shining through effortlessly.

FIND YOUR WHY: YOUR INCARNATION CROSS

Your Incarnation Cross is made up of the four most important Gates (gifts) in your chart and derived from the positions of the Sun (⊙) and Earth (⊕) in both your conscious and unconscious design. These are the top two Gates in each column.

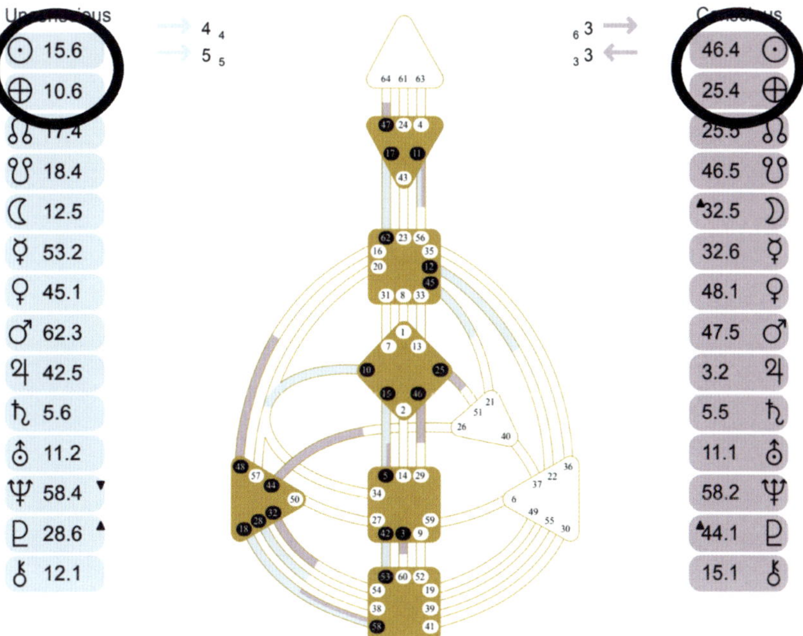

CONSCIOUS SUN GATE: This is the most important Gate in your entire chart and makes up the core of your life theme. It is quite literally how you are designed to express your light in the world, so it is potent!

CONSCIOUS EARTH GATE: This Gate grounds you and provides balance. It's what keeps you steady as you express your purpose.

UNCONSCIOUS SUN GATE: This is another potent Gate, but it can be unconscious for most.

UNCONSCIOUS EARTH GATE: This Gate is another grounding point that can be unconscious for most.

For example, in In the chart on page 209, this person has Gate 46 in their conscious sun and Gate 25 in their conscious earth (right side of the chart) and Gate 15 in their unconscious sun and Gate 10 in their unconscious earth (left side of the chart).

Looking at your own chart, what are your four Gates?

⊙ **CONSCIOUS SUN:** ______________________

⊕ **CONSCIOUS EARTH:** ______________________

⊙ **UNCONSCIOUS SUN:** ______________________

⊕ **UNCONSCIOUS EARTH:** ______________________

The Three Angles of Incarnation Crosses

Now that you know your four Gates, you can determine whether your Incarnation Cross is classified as a *Right Angle*, *Left Angle*, or *Juxtaposition*, which reveals how your purpose plays out in the world and whether it's personal, interpersonal, or fixed. This is determined from your Profile (your personality) in chapter 4.

Circle yours below.

If your Profile is a	1/3	1/4	2/4	2/5	
	3/5	3/6	or	4/6	you are a **Right Angle**
If your Profile is a	5/1	5/2	6/2	6/3	you are a **Left Angle**
If your Profile is a	4/1				you are a **Juxtaposition**

Now that you know the Gates that make up your Incarnation Cross and the angle, fill it in below.

MY INCARNATION CROSS IS ______________________________
(right angle/left angle/juxtaposition)

OF ______________________________.

Right Angle Cross

Personal Destiny

FOCUS: Self-discovery and personal karma
WHO IT AFFECTS: Primarily you
HOW IT WORKS:

- If you have a Right Angle Cross, you are here for your own personal journey and self-exploration.
- Your impact on others is more indirect—you live your purpose simply by being yourself.
- You are not responsible for influencing or guiding others; instead, your life is about experiencing and learning for yourself.
- You don't carry past-life karma or obligations to others.

For example, someone with a Right Angle Cross may feel fulfilled simply by living authentically, following what excites them, and growing as a person.

Left Angle Cross

Transpersonal Destiny

FOCUS: Interacting with and influencing others
WHO IT AFFECTS: You and others
HOW IT WORKS:

- If you have a Left Angle Cross, you are here to impact others and exchange karma (karmic relationships).

- You will meet people who are part of your soul contracts, and your purpose is often revealed through connections and interactions.
- Your life is less about personal fulfillment and more about guiding, teaching, or affecting people in some way.
- Past-life karma may play a role in your experiences.

For example, someone with a Left Angle Cross may find themselves in situations where they naturally take on a mentor role, experience deep karmic relationships, or feel a pull toward sharing with others.

Juxtaposition Cross

Fixed Destiny

FOCUS: A unique, self-contained path
WHO IT AFFECTS: Primarily you, but in a very specific way
HOW IT WORKS:

- If you have a Juxtaposition Cross, you have a very fixed, specific life path.
- You don't have personal karma like Right Angle Crosses, nor do you have karmic connections like Left Angle Crosses.
- Your life unfolds in a consistent, stable way—you are here to walk a particular path, and nothing will really change that.
- You are designed to hold a frequency rather than be deeply influenced by others.

For example, someone with a Juxtaposition Cross may feel like they've always had a clear direction and they don't deviate much from it. They may not feel heavily influenced by personal growth (like Right Angles) or relationships (like Left Angles)—they just are who they are.

Understanding Your Energetic Purpose

There are 192 different Incarnation Crosses when you include all the Gate variations, but many of them carry the same energetic theme. We've compiled a simplified list of the crosses and their core purpose, combining variations under one name for clarity. You won't need the four Gate numbers for this, just the name of the cross. Take a moment to find yours.

Incarnation Cross	Purpose
RIGHT ANGLE CROSS OF THE SPHINX	*Your purpose is to guide others toward all that is possible.*
RIGHT ANGLE CROSS OF EXPLANATION	*Your purpose is to explain things in a genius way.*
RIGHT ANGLE CROSS OF CONTAGION	*Your purpose is to inspire others through your enthusiastic energy.*
RIGHT ANGLE CROSS OF THE SLEEPING PHOENIX	*Your purpose is to stay busy doing things that ignite your soul.*
RIGHT ANGLE CROSS OF PLANNING	*Your purpose is to contribute to your community and plan for success.*
RIGHT ANGLE CROSS OF CONSCIOUSNESS	*Your purpose is to raise the consciousness of the world.*
RIGHT ANGLE CROSS OF RULERSHIP	*Your purpose is to be a natural leader.*
RIGHT ANGLE CROSS OF EDEN	*Your purpose is to explore the world and find paradise.*
RIGHT ANGLE CROSS OF THE VESSEL OF LOVE	*Your purpose is to be universally loving to all things.*
RIGHT ANGLE CROSS OF SERVICE	*Your purpose is to serve people through organization and leadership.*
RIGHT ANGLE CROSS OF TENSION	*Your purpose is to push people into new ways of thinking.*
RIGHT ANGLE CROSS OF PENETRATION	*Your purpose is to follow your ambitions and get straight to the point.*
RIGHT ANGLE CROSS OF MAYA	*Your purpose is to notice the small details and share them with others.*

Incarnation Cross	Purpose
RIGHT ANGLE CROSS OF LAWS	*Your purpose is to set rules and create laws for organization.*
RIGHT ANGLE CROSS OF THE UNEXPECTED	*Your purpose is to support others and handle the unexpected for them.*
RIGHT ANGLE CROSS OF THE FOUR WAYS	*Your purpose is to make sure others are taken care of.*
LEFT ANGLE CROSS OF MASKS	*Your purpose is to take the lead, give direction, and follow through greatly.*
LEFT ANGLE CROSS OF REVOLUTION	*Your purpose is to create change for the common good.*
LEFT ANGLE CROSS OF INDUSTRY	*Your purpose is to be productive with things you are passionate about.*
LEFT ANGLE CROSS OF SPIRIT	*Your purpose is to fuel your spirit with the pleasures that feel good to you.*
LEFT ANGLE CROSS OF MIGRATION	*Your purpose is to break free from what everyone else is doing.*
LEFT ANGLE CROSS OF DOMINION	*Your purpose is to step in and be a powerful leader.*
LEFT ANGLE CROSS OF INFORMING	*Your purpose is to hold space for others to be vulnerable for the greater good.*
LEFT ANGLE CROSS OF THE PLANE	*Your purpose is to be an earthly guide for others to tap into their intuition.*
LEFT ANGLE CROSS OF HEALING	*Your purpose is to embody and heal others through love and wellness.*
LEFT ANGLE CROSS OF UPHEAVAL	*Your purpose is to stir things up in an effort to make the world better.*
LEFT ANGLE CROSS OF ENDEAVOR	*Your purpose is to inspire depth and make big things happen in the world.*
LEFT ANGLE CROSS OF THE CLARION	*Your purpose is to bring intuitive change to those who are ready.*
LEFT ANGLE CROSS OF LIMITATION	*Your purpose is to bring structure and clarity to others.*
LEFT ANGLE CROSS OF WISHES	*Your purpose is to lead change through your wish for a better future.*

Incarnation Cross	Purpose
LEFT ANGLE CROSS OF ALIGNMENT	*Your purpose is to shift from old thinking and align with the new.*
LEFT ANGLE CROSS OF INCARNATION	*Your purpose is to observe cycles and guide others through change.*
LEFT ANGLE CROSS OF DEFIANCE	*Your purpose is to defy the odds and embody self-expression.*
LEFT ANGLE CROSS OF DEDICATION	*Your purpose is to teach in an insightful and explanatory way.*
LEFT ANGLE CROSS OF UNCERTAINTY	*Your purpose is to bring awareness to life's uncertainties.*
LEFT ANGLE CROSS OF DUALITY	*Your purpose is to find a balance between being an individual and a part of your community.*
LEFT ANGLE CROSS OF IDENTIFICATION	*Your purpose is to draw others toward worthy causes.*
LEFT ANGLE CROSS OF SEPARATION	*Your purpose is to accept and love others who are different from you.*
LEFT ANGLE CROSS OF CONFRONTATION	*Your purpose is to confront what isn't working and bring justice.*
LEFT ANGLE CROSS OF EDUCATION	*Your purpose is to encourage the importance of education.*
LEFT ANGLE CROSS OF PREVENTION	*Your purpose is to lovingly prevent others from harmful situations.*
LEFT ANGLE CROSS OF DEMANDS	*Your purpose is to demand action for what isn't working in society.*
LEFT ANGLE CROSS OF INDIVIDUALISM	*Your purpose is to push people toward their individual purpose.*
LEFT ANGLE CROSS OF CYCLES	*Your purpose is to handle the ever-changing cycles of life seamlessly.*
LEFT ANGLE CROSS OF OBSCURATION	*Your purpose is to examine life and bring new concepts to the collective.*
LEFT ANGLE CROSS OF DISTRACTION	*Your purpose is to distract others from life's worries.*
LEFT ANGLE CROSS OF THE ALPHA	*Your purpose is to take care of others through your natural leadership.*

Incarnation Cross	Purpose
LEFT ANGLE CROSS OF REFINEMENT	*Your purpose is to refine the world in an upgraded way.*
JUXTAPOSITION OF LISTENING	*Your purpose is to be an attentive listener.*
JUXTAPOSITION OF PRINCIPLES	*Your purpose is to stand up for human rights.*
JUXTAPOSITION OF FATES	*Your purpose is to be intensely driven and passionate in life.*
JUXTAPOSITION OF MOODS	*Your purpose is to focus your energy in a deep and detailed way.*
JUXTAPOSITION OF BARGAINS	*Your purpose is to make deals and bargains with others.*
JUXTAPOSITION OF DOUBTS	*Your purpose is to question things and process them logically.*
JUXTAPOSITION OF GRACE	*Your purpose is to offer grace and attention to others through listening.*
JUXTAPOSITION OF CRISIS	*Your purpose is to create intimate spaces for the people you love.*
JUXTAPOSITION OF INNOCENCE	*Your purpose is to influence the world through your love of life.*
JUXTAPOSITION OF OPINIONS	*Your purpose is to offer your opinion.*
JUXTAPOSITION OF CONTROL	*Your purpose is to bring innovation by taking control of certain situations.*
JUXTAPOSITION OF SHOCK	*Your purpose is to shock others out of complacency.*
JUXTAPOSITION OF COMPLETION	*Your purpose is to complete things that others have given up on.*
JUXTAPOSITION OF MUTATION	*Your purpose is to bring change to current rules or laws.*
JUXTAPOSITION OF CARING	*Your purpose is to bring a sense of caring to all people and things.*
JUXTAPOSITION OF RATIONALIZATION	*Your purpose is to comprehend confusing concepts.*
JUXTAPOSITION OF THE DRIVER	*Your purpose is to understand complex concepts and old patterns to lead others.*
JUXTAPOSITION OF ASSIMILATION	*Your purpose is to bring individual ideas forward to create change.*

Incarnation Cross	Purpose
JUXTAPOSITION OF CONTRIBUTION	*Your purpose is to contribute to society through demonstration.*
JUXTAPOSITION OF THE NOW	*Your purpose is to embody the gift of staying present.*
JUXTAPOSITION OF EXPERIMENTATION	*Your purpose is to be fiercely determined to achieve your goals.*
JUXTAPOSITION OF EXPERIENCE	*Your purpose is to seek out very specific and unique experiences in life.*
JUXTAPOSITION OF POSSESSION	*Your purpose is to influence and guide important people in your life.*
JUXTAPOSITION OF ARTICULATION	*Your purpose is to articulate words with love for positive change.*
JUXTAPOSITION OF EXTREMES	*Your purpose is to embrace extreme ways of living.*
JUXTAPOSITION OF STILLNESS	*Your purpose is to give wise advice or ideas when asked for.*
JUXTAPOSITION OF PROVOCATION	*Your purpose is to intuitively provoke others to change.*
JUXTAPOSITION OF BEGINNINGS	*Your purpose is to take on projects and complete them successfully.*
JUXTAPOSITION OF DETAIL	*Your purpose is to contribute ideas in a detailed way.*
JUXTAPOSITION OF STIMULATION	*Your purpose is to follow the adrenaline and thrills in life.*
JUXTAPOSITION OF INFLUENCE	*Your purpose is to influence the world through your persistence.*
JUXTAPOSITION OF RETREAT	*Your purpose is to create sacred spaces for people to be themselves.*
JUXTAPOSITION OF INTERACTION	*Your purpose is to be a leader, whether directly or indirectly.*
JUXTAPOSITION OF FORMULIZATION	*Your purpose is to lay the foundation for patterns and formulas.*
JUXTAPOSITION OF COMMITMENT	*Your purpose is to have powerful devotion to your passions.*
JUXTAPOSITION OF STRATEGY	*Your purpose is to understand relationship dynamics.*
JUXTAPOSITION OF DENIAL	*Your purpose is to be a voice of concern when things get out of hand.*

Incarnation Cross	Purpose
JUXTAPOSITION OF CONFUSION	*Your purpose is to be an objective thinker and narrate life's events.*
JUXTAPOSITION OF OPPRESSION	*Your purpose is to bring new ideas to the world for others to complete.*
JUXTAPOSITION OF CONFLICT	*Your purpose is to find joy in networking and establishing friendships.*
JUXTAPOSITION OF SERENDIPITY	*Your purpose is to enjoy the magic of how life perfectly falls into place.*
JUXTAPOSITION OF CORRECTION	*Your purpose is to correct patterns and discover a more joyful life.*
JUXTAPOSITION OF DEPTH	*Your purpose is to inspire others through depth.*
JUXTAPOSITION OF INTUITION	*Your purpose is to intuitively read others in times of need.*
JUXTAPOSITION OF CONSERVATION	*Your purpose is to conserve and preserve life.*
JUXTAPOSITION OF VALUES	*Your purpose is to establish order through rules and values.*
JUXTAPOSITION OF RISKS	*Your purpose is to take and enjoy the adrenaline of risks.*
JUXTAPOSITION OF ALERTNESS	*Your purpose is to recognize what is about to happen before it happens.*
JUXTAPOSITION OF SELF-EXPRESSION	*Your purpose is to be different and do your own unique thing.*
JUXTAPOSITION OF INSIGHT	*Your purpose is to put abstract information together to create powerful insights.*
JUXTAPOSITION OF EMPOWERING	*Your purpose is to feel empowered through happiness and security.*
JUXTAPOSITION OF POWER	*Your purpose is to bring big powerful, soulful energy to everything you do.*
JUXTAPOSITION OF FOCUS	*Your purpose is to be hyper focused in a calm way.*
JUXTAPOSITION OF HABITS	*Your purpose is to follow routines and rituals that enhance your life.*
JUXTAPOSITION OF THE TRICKSTER	*Your purpose is to rally others around new ideas and get them excited.*

Incarnation Cross	Purpose
JUXTAPOSITION OF IDEAS	*Your purpose is to express your ideas about humanity in a philosophical way.*
JUXTAPOSITION OF BEHAVIOUR	*Your purpose is to guide and correct the behavior of others for the better.*
JUXTAPOSITION OF VITALITY	*Your purpose is to bring energy to logical thinking.*
JUXTAPOSITION OF OPPOSITION	*Your purpose is to be a natural skeptic and push others to think differently.*
JUXTAPOSITION OF AMBITION	*Your purpose is to be fiercely ambitious until your dreams are a reality.*
JUXTAPOSITION OF THINKING	*Your purpose is to understand how things work and move it along.*
JUXTAPOSITION OF LIMITATION	*Your purpose is to follow the rules and preserve tradition.*
JUXTAPOSITION OF FANTASY	*Your purpose is to spot trends and fantasize about aesthetics.*
JUXTAPOSITION OF NEED	*Your purpose is to be creative and expressive in your own way.*

HOW TO BRING THIS INTO YOUR DAILY LIFE

Here's the thing—your Incarnation Cross isn't something you become or try to fit into. It's not designed to be actionable; it's just something that plays out naturally in your life whether you try to surface it or not.

For example, my Cross is the Left Angle Cross of Defiance, which is all about challenging the status quo and going against the grain. My parents would be the first to tell you that I've never done anything conventionally. They love to tell the story of the time my dad picked me up from daycare, shocked to find me wearing the most bizarre outfit he'd ever seen. When he called my mom, wondering how she let me leave the house like that, she just laughed and said, "She's a free spirit. She wanted to express herself differently today."

Similarly, I've often noticed myself rejecting the latest pop culture trends. I remember when the Twilight series came out, every girl my age went gaga over it, but I had a deep-seated opposition to it. I just had to go against popular opinion, for no reason other than a desire to be different and go against the norm. That's my defiant nature.

Another example is the work I'm doing. I've opted out of the traditional nine-to-five career path to pursue a more spiritual, entrepreneurial one. Perhaps because I felt a deeper calling to this work, or maybe because I simply don't like being told what to do!

These are just some of the many moments where I pushed boundaries, embraced my individuality, thought outside the box, or expressed myself in unconventional ways.

As you can see, your Incarnation Cross isn't something you need to chase or strive for actively—it's simply the energy you're here to embody by leaning in to the other parts of your Human Design. Therefore, the more aligned you are with your Energy Type, Strategy, and Authority, the more naturally your Incarnation Cross will unfold. Think of the Gates that make up your Incarnation Cross as added color to how this theme plays out within you.

Exercise

Now go back to the Gates chapter on page 153. Find the four Gates your Incarnation Cross is made up of to fill in the following.

My conscious sun is in Gate ________, which represents ____________________.

My conscious earth is in Gate ________, which represents ____________________.

My unconscious sun is in Gate ________, which represents ____________________.

My unconscious earth is in Gate ________, which represents ____________________.

How do you feel like each of these Gates plays out in your life? Can you think of any specific examples?

LET'S REVIEW YOUR ANGLE: I'M A . . .

- ◯ **RIGHT ANGLE**, which means my life path involves being totally immersed in deep self-exploration and learning to live as authentically as possible. My experiences and wisdom are meant to inspire the rest of the world to grow. Tip: Focus on yourself and your experiences.
- ◯ **LEFT ANGLE**, which means my purpose is about my role in other people's lives. My life path involves serving and connecting with others to change their lives. Seemingly insignificant encounters are valuable to my purpose in spreading truths of the world. I am meant to transform personal wisdom into collective wisdom. Tip: Be open to relationships and interactions that shape your purpose.
- ◯ **JUXTAPOSITION ANGLE**, which means I am meant to have a concrete path in life that I am not designed to be pulled off of. My life path involves deeply exploring my personal process and sharing understanding with my community. It is meant to be steadfast and influence others. Tip: Trust that your path is set, and you are here to hold your unique energy.

Reflection

Let's reflect on how your Incarnation Cross has played out in your life.

Are there any particular moments in your life that reflect how your angle shows up?

How has your Incarnation Cross appeared in your career, relationships, or daily life?

How does understanding your Incarnation Cross affect your perception of yourself or your life's purpose?

"As you align more closely with your innate energy and intuition, you'll naturally start to notice these aspects of your design reveal themselves."

CHAPTER 10

GOING DEEPER

Now that we are further along in your journey, let's get into a deeper and more intricate aspect of your chart: your Variables. This level of Human Design sheds light on how your body and brain thrive, offering insights into your optimal functioning.

Variables come from the arrows on both sides of your BodyGraph, so keep that handy as we dive into your Variables!

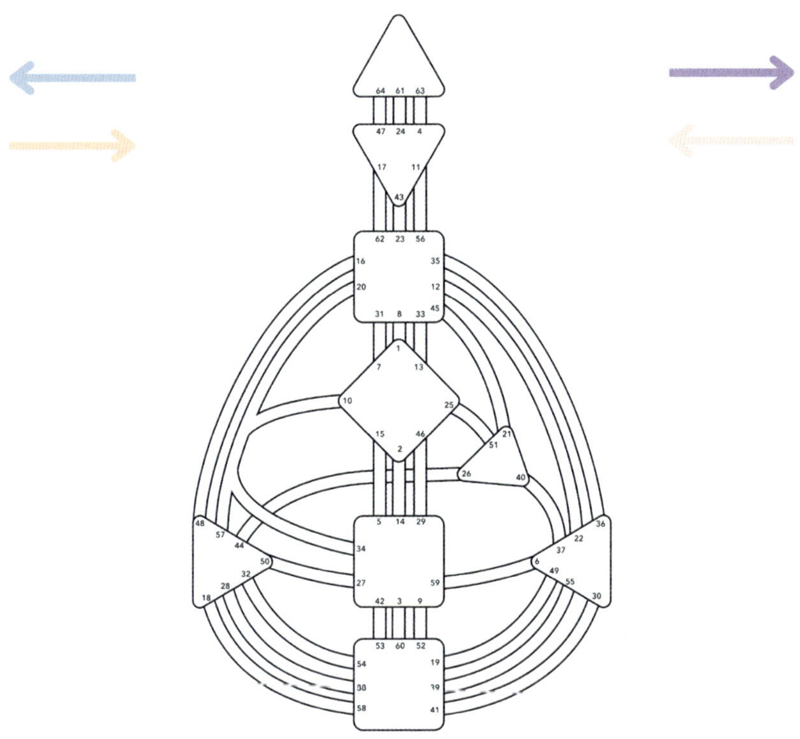

The top left arrow tells us how we best digest food and information.
The bottom left arrow tells us what environments we thrive in.
The bottom right arrow tells us how our brain views the world.
The top right arrow tells us how our brain is motivated.

It's essential to understand that Variables aren't the starting point in Human Design. These are advanced insights best explored once you've been consistently living in alignment with your Strategy and Authority. As you align more closely with your innate energy and intuition, you'll naturally start to notice these aspects of your design reveal themselves.

Variables unfold in layers, starting with Digestion and your Strongest Sense, which you are likely to notice before the age of thirty. Beyond this age, you'll likely see other aspects of your Variables manifest more fully as you grow and evolve. This gradual unfolding is why these elements of your design are best understood and integrated over time. I included this section so that when you want to dive deeper, you'll have all the insights to do so!

Digestion

Digestion, often called "determination," speaks to how our bodies best digest food and information. By eating in alignment with our design, we tend to have a clearer mind, better digestion, and more nourishment, and overall, we begin to feel better. There are twelve different Digestions, and you'll have just one of them.

Reference your chart list on page 32 for your Digestion.

MY DIGESTION IS ______________________.

SIMPLE AND PURE

CONSECUTIVE APPETITE

They digest best by eating one simple food at a time, in a specific sequence, without mixing ingredients.

Tips:

- Eat meals with a single ingredient or one main food group at a time.
- Avoid mixing too many flavors at once.
- Plan meals with one primary ingredient featured.

ALTERNATING APPETITE

They digest best by alternating among a few simple, separate foods during a meal.

Tips:

- Include various small dishes in your meals to choose from.
- Try a tapas-style dining experience for variety.
- Mix textures and flavors for a diverse eating experience.

PARTICULAR AND SEASONAL

OPEN TASTE

They thrive when they try different foods and discover what works through direct tasting and experimentation.

Tips:

- Be open to sampling before committing—your body will know what works.
- Try a variety of foods to see what your body actually likes.

CLOSED TASTE

They digest best when they stick to familiar favorites and repeat meals they love.

Tips:

- Identify foods that consistently feel good for your body and stick with them.
- Trust yourself—if you know you don't want it, don't force yourself to try it.
- Eat seasonal foods.

TEMPERATURE AND LIQUIDS

HOT THIRST

Their body is activated by warm or cooked foods, ideally served above body temperature.

Tips:

- Drink a hot beverage before or with your meals, like herbal tea or warm water.
- Incorporate warming spices such as cinnamon, ginger, or garlic into your dishes to enhance their heat.
- Let cooler foods come to room temperature before consuming.

COLD THIRST

Their digestion works best with food that is raw, cool, or below body temperature.

Tips:

- Keep a water bottle with you and sip on cold water throughout the day.
- Cool, raw foods like smoothies or salads are easiest for your body to process.

- Let hot foods cool down before eating if you don't feel drawn to warmth.

SURROUNDING ENERGY

CALM TOUCH

They digest best in peaceful, quiet environments with minimal stimulation.
Tips:

- Create a dedicated and serene dining area.
- Avoid eating when stressed or in a rush.
- Practice mindful eating to fully engage with the experience.

NERVOUS TOUCH

They digest best when there is movement or stimulation around them—like walking, talking, or eating on the go.
Tips:

- Eat in more social settings or where there is mild activity.
- You don't have to sit still to eat—do what keeps your energy flowing.
- Use mealtimes as an opportunity for engaging discussions.

NOISE LEVELS

HIGH SOUND

Their digestion is supported by pleasing, lively sounds or music while eating.
Tips:

- Play music in the background during meals.
- Consider occasionally dining out in lively environments.
- Use apps that simulate ambient sounds if eating alone.

LOW SOUND

They digest best in soft, quiet, or even silent environments.

Tips:

- Eat in a quiet place, away from bustling areas of your home or office.
- Use noise-canceling headphones if needed.
- Choose restaurants that are known for their tranquil ambience.

TIMES OF DAY AND LIGHT

DIRECT LIGHT

They digest best during the day while the sun is up, ideally with access to natural light.

Tips:

- Try to align mealtimes with daylight hours.
- If indoors, choose seats by windows or in well-lit areas.
- Opt for outdoor dining whenever possible to maximize light exposure.

INDIRECT LIGHT

They digest best in the evening or nighttime, with dim lighting and after the sun has set.

Tips:

- Use dimmable lights in your dining area to create a more subdued ambience.
- Let yourself snack at night if you're hungry—it's how your system works best.
- Choose curtains or shades that can soften bright lights during mealtimes.

Reflection

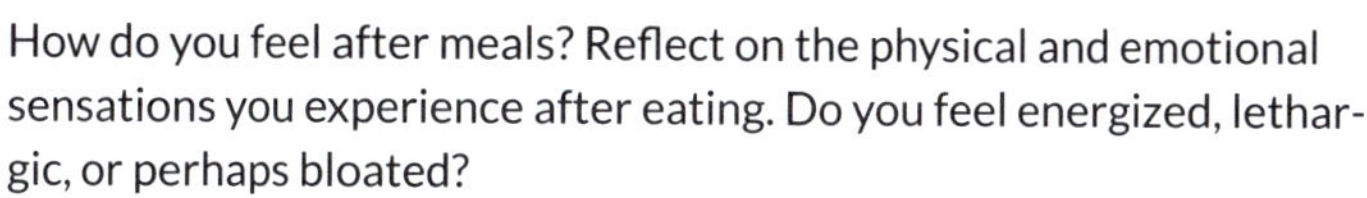
How do you feel after meals? Reflect on the physical and emotional sensations you experience after eating. Do you feel energized, lethargic, or perhaps bloated?

What adjustments could you make to support your Digestion?

What misconceptions might others have about your eating preferences and needs?

Strongest Sense

Your Strongest Sense, often referred to as "cognition," gives insight into how you may discern and understand the world around you. Think of it like a sixth sense. Our Strongest Sense supports our body in digesting food (with your Digestion), but also in choosing relationships and opportunities. There are six different Strongest Senses, and each person has one predominant sense.

Reference your chart list on page 32 for your Strongest Sense.

MY STRONGEST SENSE IS ______________________.

SMELL

Your superpower is your ability to sniff things out, whether people, opportunities, or food. You have a sensitive nose that can detect what is good—or not—for you. This sense helps you navigate your environment intuitively.

Tips:

- Surround yourself with scents you love, such as essential oils or your favorite meals.
- Before trying something new, give it a sniff to see if it "smells right."
- Use your sense of smell to aid your intuition and decision-making.

TASTE

You have a refined ability to taste and enjoy the subtleties in different flavors. This sensitivity extends beyond food to all areas of life, influencing your judgment about people, places, and experiences.

Tips:

- Pay attention to how different flavors affect your mood and choices.
- Trust when something leaves a "bad taste"—it's likely a signal to steer clear.
- Enhance your experiences by choosing flavors and foods that genuinely satisfy you.

OUTER VISION

Your cognition is strongly influenced by what you see. You appreciate aesthetics and are sensitive to the visual details of your surroundings, which can profoundly affect your mood and energy.

Tips:

- Create visually appealing environments that inspire and energize you.
- Notice and adjust anything in your surroundings that doesn't please your eye.
- Use your natural inclination toward beauty to enhance your personal and professional spaces.

INNER VISION

You have a vibrant inner world, rich with visual and sensory imagery. This cognition processes information through mental pictures and scenarios.

Tips:

- Regularly practice visualization to enhance creativity and problem-solving.
- Engage in meditation or quiet reflection to connect with your inner vision.
- Trust your inner sight to guide you in decisions and during creative processes.

FEELING

Your primary cognitive strength lies in your ability to feel your way through life. You are highly intuitive and sensitive to the energies around you, often knowing things without knowing how you know them.
Tips:

- Trust your feelings, especially when they are strong or persistent.
- Explore and express your emotions through creative outlets like music or art.
- Allow your senses to guide you in making decisions that feel right, even if they defy logic.

TOUCH

Touch is your gateway to understanding and interacting with the world. You gain insights and information through physical contact, which can make you particularly hands-on in both personal and professional contexts.
Tips:

- Incorporate tactile elements into your daily life, whether through clothing, furnishings, or activities like gardening.
- Use your hands to connect with others, through gestures like handshakes or hugs, to enhance interpersonal relations.
- Engage in activities that allow you to work with your hands, such as cooking or crafting, as this can be both fulfilling and informative.

Reflection

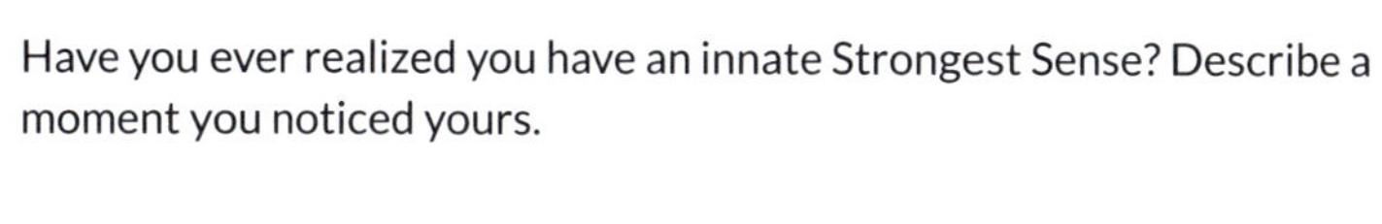

Have you ever realized you have an innate Strongest Sense? Describe a moment you noticed yours.

Do you ever use your Strongest Sense when making decisions? This can enhance your intuitive Authority.

In what ways can you further develop your Strongest Sense to enhance your personal growth?

Environment

Environment speaks to what surroundings our bodies thrive best in. By getting into the right Environment, we experience more ease and flow in our lives. There are six different Environments that shed light on how we can adjust our surroundings to enhance our well-being. It's important to remember that these Environments are represented symbolically by natural and familiar settings. For instance, if your Environment is categorized as "Caves," it doesn't mean you should literally move into a cave. Let's explore each one and look at practical tips on how you can adapt your space to resonate with your design!

Reference your chart list on page 32 for your Environment.

MY ENVIRONMENT IS ____________________.

CAVES

You prefer cozy, controlled Environments where you feel safe and protected. These settings allow you to manage your surroundings and create a sanctuary for yourself.

Tips:

- Make your living space a comfortable retreat that reflects your personal tastes and needs.
- Choose seating in public places that offers a view of the entrances and exits, providing a sense of security.
- You may want to drive to where you are going so you can leave when you want.
- Customize your work and home Environments to optimize comfort and control, like adjusting lighting and choosing your favorite decor.

MARKETS

You're at your best in bustling places where choices abound and people gather for a common purpose, much like a lively market. The energy of these spaces fuels you, and you love the buzz of potential in every corner.

Tips:

- Seek out places that pulse with energy—farmers markets, vibrant shopping districts, and busy craft fairs.
- At home, create little zones for everything important—keys here, books there. It's like setting up your own mini market!
- Build relationships at work where the exchange of ideas is as vibrant as a marketplace. Opt for jobs that let you mingle, choose, and feel the communal vibe.

KITCHENS

As a hub of creativity and energy, kitchens or similar Environments suit you best, where there is constant movement, creation, and interaction.

Tips:

- Immerse yourself in vibrant spaces where creativity is in the air—think bustling coffee shops, innovative office spaces, or your own lively kitchen.
- When relaxing, choose movies or shows that spotlight creativity—like scenes of cooking, home renovations, or artistic makeovers. These visuals resonate deeply with you and fuel your own creative spirit.
- Host gatherings or collaborative projects that bring people together to create and share.
- Make your kitchen, or another place in your home, your experiment lab—play with flavors, try new recipes, and revel in the joy of cooking. It's your playground, after all!

MOUNTAINS

Elevated spaces that provide a broad perspective are ideal for you. You thrive in Environments where you can oversee everything and gain insight from a heightened vantage point.

Tips:

- Seek out high places like hilltops, upper floors of buildings, or anywhere you can get a clear, expansive view.
- Arrange your workspace so that it gives you a sense of overview—perhaps near a window that looks out over an open area.
- Travel to places that allow you to stand back and take in the scenery, offering new perspectives and inspirations.

VALLEYS

You thrive in Environments where connections are easy and everything feels within reach, just like a valley that's open and inviting. You love being in the mix, close to the action where life unfolds.

Tips:

- Choose a home in the heart of it all, where coffee shops, stores, and parks are just a short stroll away.
- Embrace places that let you soak in the sounds and scenes around you—these feed your soul and spark your connections.
- Travel to locations that keep you connected to the earth and the people on it. Think road trips or exploring new neighborhoods on foot.

SHORES

Your ideal setting is at the edge of a space, where you can enjoy both the tranquility of a boundary and the liveliness of nearby activity. This might be a literal shoreline or a more metaphoric one, like the edge of any community or busy area.

Tips:

- Seek out places where you can observe activity without being overwhelmed by it.
- Enjoy the transition areas in nature, such as where the forest meets a field, the land meets the water, or the suburbs border a city.
- Position yourself in social or professional settings where you can easily engage or retreat as needed.

How do you feel in your current Environment? Does it energize you, relax you, or possibly even stress you out?

Reflection

What changes can you make in your personal or professional spaces to better align with your ideal Environment?

How can you communicate your environmental preferences to others to improve your interactions and shared spaces?

Environment Style and Movement

Along with our Environment, we also have an Environment Style, which gives us insight into the role we naturally adopt in our surroundings. We can either observe or be observed. This also gives us a look into how we may move our bodies best. You'll find this in the direction of your bottom left arrow.

⟵ IF YOUR BOTTOM LEFT ARROW POINTS LEFT . . .

You take on an "observed" role in your Environments. This means you really come alive in places where there's lots to do and see. Think of yourself as kind of a natural star—people tend to notice you, and honestly, you kind of enjoy the attention.

Your happy place is all about those vibrant, lively Environments. Whether it's a bustling gym, a fun party, or a busy work scene, if it's high-energy, you are likely going to enjoy being there!

When it comes to movement, you may enjoy moving your body regularly and exercising often. Moving and grooving is your vibe.

⟶ IF YOUR BOTTOM LEFT ARROW POINTS RIGHT . . .

You take on an "observer" role in your Environments. This means you enjoy those calm, chill environments where you can just relax and take it all in. Watching the world go by is your jam.

Your happy place is a quiet spot where you can unwind. It might be a peaceful park, a quiet beach, or the corner of a cozy café. Chill vibes only.

When it comes to movement, it is important to not force a routine or rigidity. You operate best in flow and tuning in to what your body needs day to day! Listening to your body is key.

View

Your View shows how your brain sees the world around you. Think of this like a veil in which you understand things. There are six different Views, and you'll have one that illustrates your natural outlook on life.

Reference your chart list on page 32 for your View.

MY VIEW IS ______________________________.

SURVIVAL VIEW

Outlook: You naturally focus on ensuring safety and security.

Tips: Trust in the stability of your life. Focus on the resources you have rather than what you're missing. This helps maintain a calm and secure mindset.

POSSIBILITY VIEW

Outlook: You see the world as a place of endless opportunities and possibilities.

Tips: Keep an optimistic view. Encourage yourself to dream big and remain open to new possibilities without getting bogged down by skepticism.

POWER VIEW

Outlook: Your focus is on dynamics of control, influence, and leadership.

Tips: Use your understanding of power constructively. Aim to empower others as well as yourself and recognize where positive leadership can make a difference.

WANTING VIEW

Outlook: You are keen on identifying what is lacking or needed.

Tips: Acknowledge areas that need improvement but balance this with appreciation for what already works well to avoid constant dissatisfaction.

PROBABILITY VIEW

Outlook: You view situations with a practical and realistic lens.

Tips: Stay grounded and practical. While it's good to be aware of limitations, don't let them deter you from pursuing achievable goals.

PERSONAL VIEW

Outlook: Your focus is on personal relevance and impact.

Tips: Stay true to what matters to you. Focus on personal growth and authenticity rather than comparing yourself to others or conforming to external expectations.

Reflection

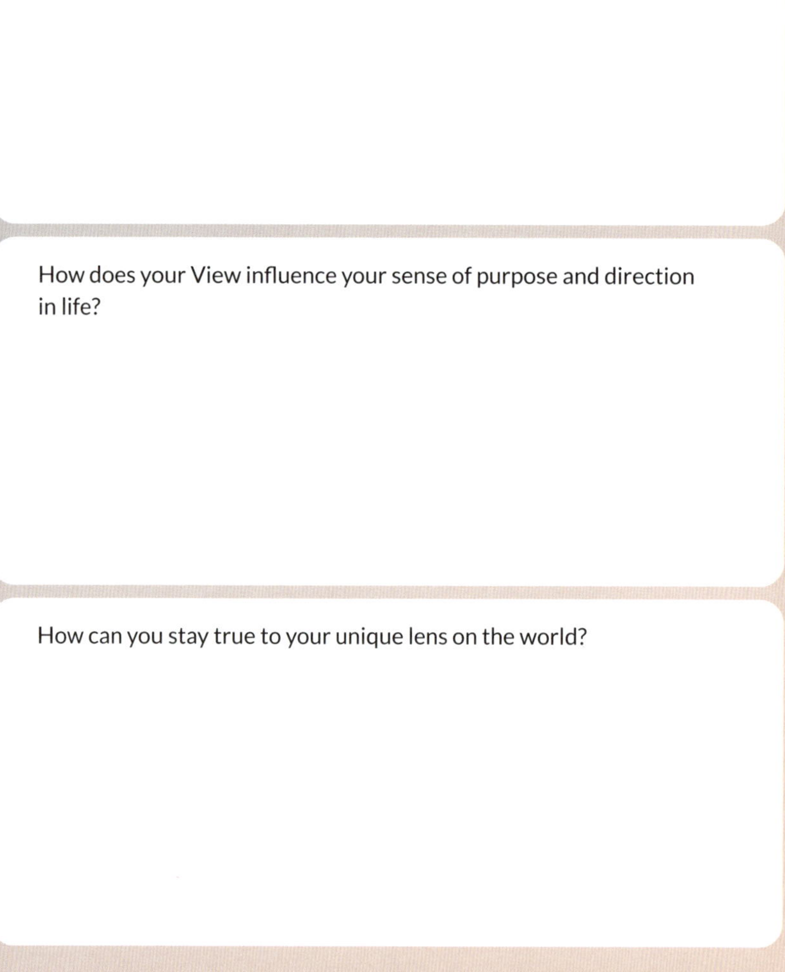

What positive outcomes have you experienced because of your natural View?

How does your View influence your sense of purpose and direction in life?

How can you stay true to your unique lens on the world?

Manifesting Style

This is an emerging concept in the Human Design community that expands on what has traditionally been called our "perspective." Each person either has a focused or peripheral Manifesting Style. We refer to Manifesting Styles as either specific (focused) or nonspecific (peripheral). Manifesting Style can tell you how you best bring your intentions to life, a.k.a. how you manifest! We find this in the direction of your bottom right arrow.

IF YOUR BOTTOM RIGHT ARROW POINTS LEFT . . .

You have a specific Manifesting Style, meaning you manifest best when you focus on specific details and clear, defined goals.

For example: When setting intentions or goals, be as detailed as possible. Envision exactly what you want, down to the smallest details, and focus on these specifics in your visualization and action steps.

IF YOUR BOTTOM RIGHT ARROW POINTS RIGHT . . .

You have a nonspecific Manifesting Style, which means you excel when you keep your intentions broad and open, focusing on the overall feeling or outcome rather than the specifics.

For example: Instead of detailing every step or aspect of what you wish to manifest, focus on the general feeling of the end result. Let the universe fill in the details and be open to receiving opportunities in various forms that align with your broader vision.

DEEPENING YOUR MANIFESTATION PRACTICE

For both styles, it's crucial to:

- Stay aligned with your true self and make sure your goals and intentions reflect your authentic desires, not what others expect of you.
- Use your Strategy and Authority when making decisions.
- Be aware of when your mind shifts from its aligned state, which can signal you are off track.
- Use affirmations and visualizations. Regularly affirm and visualize your goals in a way that aligns with your Manifesting Style to reinforce your intentions and keep your energy focused.

and applying your Manifesting Style can profoundly impact your effectiveness in manifesting. When I learned mine, it changed the game for me. I started getting ultra specific about what I desired, including timelines, vivid descriptions, names, colors, etc. I'm convinced this is how I manifested my husband. I wrote the most specific description of his personality traits, overall vibe, and family. And he showed up just on time!

Motivation

Motivation speaks to how our mind perceives information. When our mind is motivated in the correct way, it is easier to go in the most aligned direction and step into our gifts with more ease. There are six different Motivations.

Reference your chart list on page 32 for your Motivation.

MY MOTIVATION IS ______________________.

FEAR

Your mind is motivated by a need to deeply understand and manage uncertainties or potential risks. For instance, when discussing investment opportunities, you're likely to probe into every potential risk, insisting on extensive research before making any commitments.

Tip: Really dive into verifying information and solidifying security measures. You naturally dig deeper into topics to soothe any doubts and build a strong, reliable knowledge base.

HOPE

Your mind is fueled by optimism and a firm belief that everything will turn out well. In challenging work scenarios, you're the one uplifting the team, focusing on potential positive outcomes and encouraging everyone to see beyond the immediate hurdles.

Tip: Keep your outlook bright and trusting. Let go of unnecessary worries by believing in the natural progression of events.

DESIRE

Your mind is driven by what you truly want to achieve or experience. You might, for example, choose a career path that resonates deeply with your passions, like starting a business centered around your love for art or environmental sustainability.

Tip: Align your daily actions with what lights you up inside. Let your true desires guide your decisions, ensuring they're channeled in ways that really matter.

NEED

Your mind is keen on pinpointing and tackling immediate needs or problems. In group projects, you're quick to identify essential tasks and organize the team's efforts efficiently.

Tip: Lean in to areas where you can make a tangible impact. Whether it's organizing, problem-solving, or offering direct help, your knack for seeing and meeting needs is invaluable.

GUILT

You're motivated by a deep-seated need to better yourself and those around you. You might find yourself spearheading community projects, driven by a strong sense of duty to utilize your abilities for the greater good.

Tip: Focus on growth and lending a hand but remember not to stretch yourself too thin. It's okay to set boundaries and avoid carrying burdens that aren't yours.

INNOCENCE

Your Motivation comes from a desire to live authentically and without pretense. Choosing to live in a tiny home, for instance, could be a way to simplify your life and align more closely with your values, rather than following the conventional path.

Tip: Stay true to yourself and your unique path. Embrace the quirks and choices that define you, leading by example rather than pushing others to change.

Motivation Mindsets

In addition to the way your mind perceives information, there are two general Motivation Mindsets—strategic and receptive. To find yours, look at the direction of the top right arrow on your chart.

← IF YOUR TOP RIGHT ARROW POINTS LEFT . . .

You're "strategic." This means you possess a natural inclination toward structured and focused thinking. You thrive on delving into details and understanding the intricacies of any subject or situation. Your approach to information is methodical and often linear, preferring to concentrate on specific topics to maintain clarity and direction. Asking questions and seeking logical solutions are part of your natural skill set. You also benefit from having personal spaces where you can retreat, rejuvenate, and recharge before stepping back into the complexities of the world.

→ IF YOUR TOP RIGHT ARROW POINTS RIGHT . . .

Your Mindset is "receptive." This means you naturally absorb information in an open and expansive manner. You're not one to dive deeply into specifics right away; instead, you let knowledge come to you organically, often realizing its depth only when others prompt you. Your strength lies in seeing the bigger picture and attuning to nuances without a predetermined agenda. This approach allows you to be highly adaptable and perceptive, though it also makes you sensitive to criticism. Creating an environment that minimizes judgment and maximizes support is crucial for you. It helps to have strategic thinkers around who can help draw out and structure the wisdom you gather.

Reflection

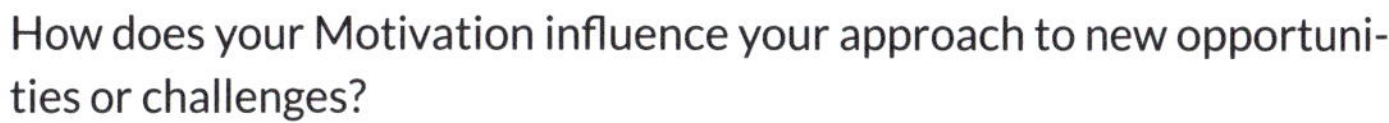

How does your Motivation influence your approach to new opportunities or challenges?

How does your Motivation Mindset (strategic or receptive) impact your learning style and information processing?

What are some past experiences where your Motivation led to significant personal growth or success?

Now that we've done a deep dive into the world of Variables, I hope you feel excited and inspired about what you've discovered. This aspect of Human Design is all about tuning in to the unique ways your body and brain work best. Think of it as learning the secret language of your own design, which opens a whole new way of living that's just waiting for you to explore. Have fun with it.

"Imagine waking up every day feeling more like yourself than ever before—connected to your energy, aligned with your purpose, and confident in your unique way of moving through the world."

CHAPTER 11

The DESIGN *of* YOU

Imagine waking up every day feeling more like yourself than ever before—connected to your energy, aligned with your purpose, and confident in your unique way of moving through the world. That's what living your Human Design is all about. It doesn't mean being perfect or trying to fit into a specific mold; it's about embracing the gifts, quirks, and strengths that make you you.

Picture this: You're a Generator who used to feel stuck and burned out because you were constantly saying yes to things that didn't excite you. Now you're following your Strategy of waiting to respond and focusing only on what lights you up. You're thriving in work you love, surrounded by people who energize you, and finally experiencing the deep satisfaction your Energy Type is designed for.

Or perhaps you're a Projector who spent years trying to keep up with the hustle culture, feeling drained and unseen. Now you're honoring your need to wait for the right invitations, and you've built a life where your insights are valued, your contributions are recognized, and your energy feels restored.

This is what's possible when you embrace your design. You don't need to force changes overnight—rather, you'll make small, intentional shifts that lead to lasting transformation.

LIVING YOUR DESIGN

Human Design isn't about rigid rules or quick fixes—it's a lifelong experiment. It means trying new strategies, reflecting on what works, and giving yourself permission to evolve. Some days, you'll feel completely in flow. Other days, you might struggle to stay aligned. That's okay. This journey is about progress, not perfection.

If you ever feel unsure, remember the alignment practices we've explored throughout this book. From honoring your Strategy to tuning in to your Authority, these tools are here to support you. Let's revisit what's possible when you live in alignment:

BEFORE ALIGNMENT	AFTER ALIGNMENT
You feel stuck, overwhelmed, and unsure of your next steps. You're constantly second-guessing yourself or seeking validation from others.	*You make decisions with ease, knowing they're right for you. Opportunities flow into your life, and you feel a sense of purpose and clarity like never before.*
You're exhausted from trying to keep up with everyone else's expectations. You're constantly chasing goals that don't truly resonate.	*You create a life that works for you—one that feels spacious, fulfilling, and deeply authentic.*
Relationships feel strained because you're not honoring your boundaries or communicating your needs.	*You attract connections that align with your energy, and you feel seen, understood, and supported.*

These are just a few of the transformations that can unfold when you trust your design. Take it one step at a time and know that every small shift brings you closer to the life you're meant to live.

BRINGING YOUR DREAM LIFE TO LIFE

As this book draws to a close, remember that each chapter has been more than just a reading experience; it's been a journey toward the deepest understanding of yourself. This is not the end, but a beautiful and powerful beginning. Now you can gather all the insights and tools you've discovered, embrace the fullness of your unique design, and use them to craft a life brimming with joy, purpose, and deep alignment.

EMBRACE THE JOURNEY OF SELF-DISCOVERY

Reflecting on my own journey with Human Design, I remember the days when I felt lost, unsure of my path and disconnected from my true purpose. Like you, I sought answers and guidance, hoping to find a way to live a life that felt genuinely mine. It was through embracing my design—understanding that I am a Generator, meant to respond rather than initiate—that I began to see the shifts. I started to say no to what drained me and yes to what invigorated and excited me. Each decision, guided by my Authority, brought me closer to the life I always dreamed of—a life where I am not just surviving but thriving.

Your journey through these pages has started the same process. From the exercises to the reflective questions, every step was designed to lead you to greater self-awareness and personal evolution. Go back to the exercises you did here and think of them as invitations—to challenge yourself, to comfort yourself, and to ultimately change yourself.

LIVE OUT YOUR UNIQUE DESIGN

Now I invite you to start living out your design, not tomorrow, not next week, but right now. Let your Strategy guide your daily actions. Let your Authority lead your decision-making. Feel the empowering clarity of knowing when something is right for you and having the courage to act on it. Recognize the strength in your Defined Centers and the wisdom in your Undefined ones. Every aspect of your Human Design is a tool, ready to assist you in navigating the complexities of life with grace and authenticity.

CRAFT A LIFE ALIGNED WITH YOUR TRUE SELF

The real power of Human Design lies in its ability to help you live out your true purpose—not a purpose imposed by others, but one that is deeply and uniquely yours. Whether it's transforming your relationships, excelling in your career, or growing in personal fulfillment, you possess all you need within you. Take another look at your vision board and see what excites you. Go back to the lists you made in chapter 5 and remember, you were designed for this. The blueprint to your dream life lies in the very fibers of your being, encoded in your design.

CONTINUE YOUR JOURNEY WITH HEART AND HOPE

Human Design is not a static experience; it is a continuous journey of discovery and growth. Each day offers new insights, new challenges, and new opportunities to align more closely with your true self. Keep this book close—not just as a reminder of what you've learned, but as a companion on your ongoing journey. And as you experiment with and refine your understanding of your design, know that each step, no matter how small, is perfect. Every adjustment, every realization, is guiding you ever closer to the vibrant, fulfilling, and purposeful life you deserve to live.

As you turn the last page, know that the story of your transformation is just beginning. Step forward with the tools you've gathered, the insights you've gained, and the dreams you've nurtured. Your design is not just a map to follow; it's a living, breathing invitation to become everything you were meant to be.

REFERENCES AND RESOURCES

REFERENCES

I found the following books to be especially helpful in my research while writing *The Design of You*.

Parkyn, Chetan. *Human Design: Discover the Person You Were Born to Be*. New World Library, 2010.

Ra Uru Hu and Lynda Bunnell. *The Definitive Book of Human Design: The Science of Differentiation*. HDC Publishing, 2011.

Rudd, Richard. *The Gene Keys: Unlocking the Higher Purpose Hidden in Your DNA*. Watkins Publishing, 2013.

RESOURCES

LOOK UP YOUR HUMAN DESIGN CHART

Discover your unique Human Design by visiting our website. Just scan the QR code and enter your details directly on our site. You'll need your full birth date, exact time of birth, and place of birth to generate an accurate chart.

LEARN MORE ABOUT HUMAN DESIGN OR BECOME A READER

Interested in going even deeper into Human Design? We offer a variety of courses and resources designed to help you master Human Design and apply it to every aspect of your life. Whether you're just starting out or looking to deepen your understanding, there's something for everyone. Check out our learning resources at our website via the QR code below.

Additionally, you can book a personal reading with one of our hand-selected Human Design Mastery–certified readers. Experience a tailored session that focuses on your unique design and provides you with actionable insights to align with your true self.

If you're ready to turn your passion for Human Design into a profession, consider joining our Human Design Mastery program. As an HDM-certified Human Design reader, you'll learn from the best, practice with real charts, and guide others on their path to personal alignment. For more details on how you can enroll and start your career as a professional Human Design reader, visit our website by scanning this QR code.

DOWNLOAD OUR APP

Explore your Human Design on the go with our mobile app! Our app makes it easy to learn about your entire chart, or your friends' charts, right from your smartphone. Download it today and start your journey to self-discovery and alignment. Scan the QR code to get started!

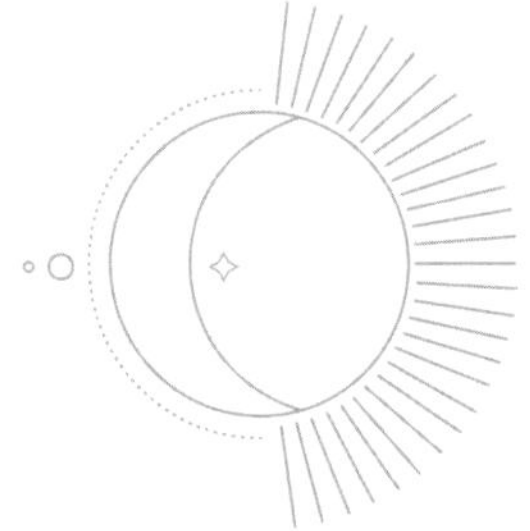

ACKNOWLEDGMENTS

My husband, Zander, for always seeing my light and believing in me the most. I wouldn't be here without your constant support, love, and encouragement.

My Reflector dogs, Gus Gus and Rupert, who both sat in my lap and at my feet for the entirety of writing this book, and who come along with me every time I teach or give a reading. You lick my tears, make me giggle, and bring me the greatest joy.

My mom, who has always seen me for exactly who I am and never asked me to change.

My beautiful students, whose enthusiasm and dedication to learning from me fills me with immense gratitude. Every session and every conversation with you all remind me why I do what I do. Thank you for your trust and for celebrating this knowledge with me.

My mentor, Emily Greene (Emily the Medium), for teaching me how to harness my spiritual gifts and connect to something beyond this realm.

My amazing team, who are the unsung heroes behind this book. During one of the most challenging periods of my life, you held everything together, allowing me the space to create and write. This book would not exist without your support.

Ra Uru Hu for enduring one heck of a ride, not only receiving the profound information of Human Design but also making it his life's work by sharing it with the rest of us. Your work has allowed me, along with thousands of others, to understand a deeper purpose in life.

ABOUT THE AUTHOR

LEAH MCCLOUD is a certified Human Design educator and the founder of The Design Of You, a place to learn all about Human Design. She has taught hundreds of students and consulted with thousands, transforming lives through the principles of Human Design. Her insights are not only drawn from extensive personal experience but are also deeply infused with her passion for spirituality, energetics, and holistic wellness. Beyond Human Design, she is a skilled psychic medium and sound healer, passionately dedicated to normalizing and celebrating spiritual gifts.

Human Design radically changed her life, compelling her to unbecome the version of herself that felt unfulfilled and step fully into her highest self. This personal transformation ignited a deep passion within her to share and teach the intricate details of Human Design.

Leah's approach is deeply practical, making complex spiritual and energetic concepts useful in everyday life. Born from years of dedicated study and practice, this book serves as an accessible guide for anyone eager to explore their potential and embrace their unique spiritual gifts.

Outside of her professional endeavors, Leah is a lover of the moon; eclectic home decor; cooking high-vibrational foods; and spending time with her husband, Zander, and their two French bulldogs. She lives her teachings, dedicating her life to exploring and embodying the principles of alignment and abundance.